# The Evolution of Leadership

Don Jones and Corky Reams

**Gotham Books**

30 N Gould St.
Ste. 20820, Sheridan, WY 82801
https://gothambooksinc.com/

Phone: 1 (307) 464-7800

© 2024 *Don Jones*. All rights reserved.

No part of this book may be reproduced, stored in a retrieval system, or transmitted by any means without the written permission of the author.

Published by Gotham Books (July 4, 2024)

ISBN: 979-8-88775-848-0 (H)
ISBN: 979-8-88775-846-6 (P)
ISBN: 979-8-88775-847-3 (E)

Because of the dynamic nature of the Internet, any web addresses or links contained in this book may have changed since publication and may no longer be valid.

The views expressed in this work are solely those of the author and do not necessarily reflect the views of the publisher, and the publisher hereby disclaims any responsibility for them.

# Contents

| | |
|---|---|
| Meet the Authors | VII |
| 1. I Lost My Shoe | 1 |
| 2. I Only Wave at My Neighbors | 5 |
| 3. I Watched the Fish Die | 11 |
| 4. I'm Dealing with Blue Flames | 15 |
| 5. I Did Not Choose Leadership | 19 |
| 6. Running at My Own Speed | 23 |
| 7. Seemingly Logical Attribute | 27 |
| 8. What Gift is in the Box? | 31 |
| 9. Are You Giving Out C.A.S.H Today | 35 |
| 10. I Don't Get in The Water | 39 |
| 11. The Joy of Spinning Wheels | 43 |
| 12. Counterfeit Feelings | 49 |
| 13. The Second Pandemic-Emptiness | 53 |
| 14. Self-Interrogation | 57 |
| 15. Could Humpty Dumpty Prevent The Fall? | 61 |
| 16. The Experience Self Violates Tradition | 65 |
| 17. I Don't Like Leaf Shine | 69 |
| 18. Avoid Uneven Pavements | 75 |

| | | |
|---|---|---|
| 19. | Whales Land on A Beach | 79 |
| 20. | It's Coming | 83 |
| 21. | Stop Eating from Baby Jars | 87 |
| 22. | Unconscious in Plain Sight | 91 |
| 23. | Perception of Reality | 95 |
| 24. | Hide-and-Seek | 101 |
| 25. | Co-Signing Silliness | 107 |
| 26. | Walking off the Playground | 111 |
| 27. | I'm in My Right Mind | 115 |
| 28. | I Want It All | 119 |
| 29. | The Mirage of Control | 123 |
| 30. | The Mind-Numbing Effects of Technology in Leadership | 125 |
| 31. | Starting at the Bottom | 129 |
| 32. | Starting at the Bottom (Cont'd) | 131 |
| 33. | A Square Peg in a Round Hole: Leading the 21st Century Employee Frontier | 133 |
| 34. | Navigating the Generational Jungle: A Leader's Hilariously Twisted Guide | 137 |
| 35. | Building Bridges, Not Walls | 139 |
| 36. | Embracing Emotions: Leading Beyond the Numbers | 143 |
| 37. | The Emotional Toolbox: Practical Strategies for a Harmonious Multi-Generational Workplace | 147 |
| 38. | "The Power of Paradox: Embracing Contradictions in Leadership" | 151 |
| 39. | Confidence, an Underutilized Co-pilot | 153 |
| 40. | Confidence Continued | 155 |

| | | |
|---|---|---|
| 41. | Experience, Insight, and Control | 161 |
| 42. | Building a Trustworthy Team | 167 |
| 43. | Building a Trustworthy Team (Cont'd) | 169 |
| 44. | AI and the Future of Leadership: Bridging the Skills Gap and Navigating Regulation | 171 |
| 45. | The Symbiosis of Leadership and Technology: Charting the Course for the Future | 175 |
| 46. | I Think the Wiring Is Wrong | 179 |

# Meet the Authors

## Don Jones

Don Jones is more than just an author; he is a visionary, an inventor, and a pioneering force in the realm of big-box retail. With a career spanning over three decades, he has witnessed the retail industry's transformation and played a crucial role in shaping its trajectory.

As an esteemed author, Jones entered the literary world marked by his incisive and transformative insights. His works offer a rich tapestry of knowledge and foresight, garnering critical acclaim. In his latest offering, *The Evolution of Leadership*, Jones delves deep into his reservoir of experience, presenting a forward-looking perspective on leadership within the dynamic landscape of retail.

Jones's influence extends beyond the confines of retail. As an inventor, his innovative contributions have reshaped not just the retail sector but also the broader business world. His book is a treasure trove of wisdom on fostering innovation and creativity, inviting readers to break conventional boundaries and catalyze positive change in their respective domains.

Imagine the unparalleled advantage of having a mentor with over thirty years of experience in big-box retail. Jones brings a wealth of knowledge, encompassing strategies and tactics proven to succeed. His insights are invaluable, whether you're a seasoned industry professional or embarking on your retail career.

Prepare to journey through the evolving landscape of leadership under the guidance of a true industry luminary. Don Jones stands as your mentor, your beacon of inspiration, and your catalyst for success in the retail world, helping you reach new pinnacles of achievement and innovation.

Welcome to *The Evolution of Leadership*. Join us on this enlightening journey as Don Jones leads the way to a new era of retail leadership and success.

## Corky Reams

With a career spanning three decades, Corky Reams has been at the forefront of shaping market trends in open market sales and business development. His journey, marked by resilience and innovation, began with significant contributions at AT&T, where he honed his skills in strategic business growth and client relations.

Corky's expertise was further solidified through his work on StudenTrac, a groundbreaking project that revolutionized attendance tracking in public schools and saved millions in attendance revenue. His role in this initiative demonstrated his technical acumen and commitment to impactful educational solutions.

Following his success with StudenTrac, Corky played a pivotal role at American Express. Here, he continued to drive substantial growth and form strategic alliances, further cementing his reputation as a business development and market expansion leader.

His career then took him to DirecTV, where he demonstrated exceptional business acumen, contributing to significant sales growth and establishing key industry partnerships. It was during this period of professional highs that Corky faced a personal health crisis.

In 2010, Corky Reams suffered a massive life-threatening heart attack at the Denver Airport. In a remarkable turn of events, he became the first patient to fully recover from the "Arctic Sun" operation in 2010. This experience did not slow him down but fueled his drive for continuous professional growth and personal resilience.

Throughout his career, Corky has been instrumental in establishing technical staffing companies and software development firms as an independent consultant. His experience spans impactful roles in both corporate and entrepreneurial sectors, demonstrating a unique perspective drawn from over thirty years of diverse business experience.

Corky offers expertise in business development, sales and marketing, strategic partnerships, staffing and recruitment, and software development. His book *The Evolution of Leadership*, co-authored with Don Jones, encapsulates these insights, providing practical knowledge for success in the ever-changing business world, particularly in response to the new AI invasion.

Outside of work, Corky is a passionate advocate for education and technology. Despite facing personal health challenges, his journey remains a testament to resilience and continuous professional growth.

# Chapter One

# I Lost My Shoe

If you operate in a brick-and-mortar building, space allocation is profoundly critical. Sales per square foot can never be forgotten. We often talk about reading the shopping cart to increase the average ticket price, but what if there is no shopping cart?

Each associate must engage every customer with a simple greeting: Good Morning, afternoon, or evening, no matter what project they are working on.

What if you tried engaging the mind before reading the cart? Your chance of driving a much higher average ticket has just increased by a factor of four. You get an opportunity to grow that average ticket four times higher with just that question.

Retail is a behavior game. Therefore, covering a bunch of numbers with the associates may not resonate with them. Remember, numbers are habits, and habits are people. Let's say you wanted to increase your transaction growth. All you need to do is change how you measure great customer service. Helping a customer with what they requested or ask of you can be revealed as giving great customer service.

Let's measure excellent service differently. What if you awarded associates for remembering the customer names? They say an average customer shops at your establishment four or five times a year. Start rewarding your associates for greeting as many customers as they can by name. You will most likely have that customer visit your location four or five times weekly.

I must admit, I was seduced by hearing my name. For example, I don't drink coffee that often. However, one morning, I decided to stop by a local coffee shop to get a cup of coffee. The associate behind the counter asked if I came by there often. I told him no, explaining that I wasn't into coffee like that; I just decided to stop by that morning to get a cup of coffee. He asked me for my name, and I told him. Before we departed, he told me he hoped to see me again, but I wasn't much of a coffee drinker.

After a few weeks had passed, I decided to stop by that coffee shop just to see if the gentleman remembered my face. He not only remembered me, but he also remembered my name. He greeted me with a "Good morning, Don. It's great to have you back."

Mind you, I'm not much of a coffee drinker, but I found myself visiting that establishment two to three times a week. Now, before you say it was the caffeine that drove me back, I can say this without hesitation—caffeine does not motivate me that way. I was seduced by hearing my name. Hearing my name made me feel my money mattered there. To hand over your hard-earned money to a stranger is difficult.

Let's change the narrative. To hand over your hard-earned money to a friend that is serving you is easy. I would drain my bank account to get this repeated feeling.

We are emotional beings. Why do people purchase high-end sports cars? It taps into their emotional being. It justifies their spending. When under pressure to make up lost ground on underperforming metrics, most leaders resort to applying pain to others, and it starts the cascading effect of making everyone below them produce that same pain to others. Many leaders will absorb that pain and go on to deliver outstanding results. Here's where leaders need to pivot in their style of managing others with pain.

Most salary leaders can and will handle turbulence with ease. If leaders are not trained to handle that pain stick, they start using it on everyone. In their mind, they think *it worked on me; therefore, it will work on everyone else.*

Losing momentum in business is challenging to deal with, and yes, you must gain immediate traction to remain relevant. The associates are your feet; you need them to run fast to get the momentum going in the right direction. Everything appears to be heading in the right direction, and you start feeling good about your pain stick and its effect on your team. You also tell yourself you are going to improve your average ticket, transactions, and margins in a short time.

Here's what's undetected to the sight: your pain stick has started to breed fear into your associates. Here's what I know about fear: fear breeds fatigue, and fatigue results in failure. My question is, why are you looking for your lost shoe when you have no feet?

Leaders must transition into a more dynamic style of leading others. I am a trained professional and can deal with turbulence and pressure with a bit of ease. In addition, I have the leadership experience to perform in those turbulent environments. Reflecting on my pilot training allowed me to perform well in this area of the business.

Here's what you need to know about the human brain. Our reasoning skills are divided into two parts: systematic and logical or unconscious and emotional. Can you imagine being unconscious and emotional as a pilot? The results are never good. With that said, I'm not telling you that no pressure is great. If you have a bleeding wound, you must apply pressure to slow or stop the bleeding. It could be the deciding factor between life and death. You just need to know when and where to apply pressure. If you respond that you're not a retail doctor, hire one to train you. That's not a valid excuse for not performing at your peak level.

You can hire an executive coach or start by reading books. I leave you with this provoking question: is your current leadership style an asset or liability?

Only you can answer this question honestly. Inspiring with the proper level of accountability is key.

# Chapter Two

# I Only Wave at My Neighbors

Who doesn't enjoy a great discount on a product? That's one of the many reasons why we shop. It's hard to walk away from a super deal. In fact, many will purchase an item even if they don't need it if it has a great discounted price. We have all been guilty of engaging in this behavior. Shopping is pleasurable, and many of us feel good when we shop. I have witnessed friends go shopping to pick their mood up.

Even after a long physically or mentally exhausting week, we often shop to feel good. You will most likely get foot traffic just by opening your doors to customers. What a wonderful thing.

Let's define a purchase; it falls into three categories: you purchase because you are repairing something that needs replacing, you are looking to enhance an existing location, or you are building something new. With the above said, you may think all you need is a building and merchandise or an online site with the right discounted merchandise. If you think in this sequence, you are partially correct. Under the right conditions and circumstances, almost anyone can win. When the wind is at your back, success is virtually a given.

Many customers will continue to frequent you due to proximity and location, and ease of shopping has advantages. Most of your customers are your (neighbors) if you have a physical building. They enter your building, and the associate greets them with "Hello. Can I help you?" or they ask, "Are you finding everything you need?"

The typical response from the customer is "Yes, I'm good," or "Can you tell me where I can locate XYZ."

You check your customer service score at the end of the week; your score is mid to high, and everything looks on the plus side. The lion's share of customers are repeat customers and will most likely tell a friend, colleague, or family member about their shopping experience.

Your financial numbers are also trending in the black, so you may think it's time to break out with the candle and cake. Let's celebrate, team! Before you light that candle, allow me to give you some scientific facts on loyal behavior and who is really thinking for us all.

It may come as a surprise to you, but what I'm about to share with you is 100 percent factual. Before I give you some data points on this topic, let me go on record and say I believe in celebrating short milestones. It's a great motivating tool to keep the team focused on winning. For example, I often celebrate by playing golf when I can stay away from butter pecan ice cream for a week; it's one of my weak points.

Remember when I said almost anyone can win when the wind is at your back? Ask any pilot how critical the wind can be when landing an airplane. From the moment you start learning to fly, you're taught to land into the wind, if possible. Undoubtedly, while you can land with tailwinds, it increases your risk of things going wrong. But at the same time, most airplanes have performance charts that let you calculate takeoffs and landings with up to ten knots of tailwind.

So, what's the big deal with tailwinds? There are two significant factors: performance and controllability of the aircraft.

Businesses operate under these same rules—performance and controllability. When the wind is not in your favor, this could have fatal consequences for the operation of your business. So, who is the wind in your business? It's your customers. When the wind shifts at the wrong time, it's never good. Customers will continue to shop with you as long as no other business opens its doors, offering the same merchandise at similar prices.

Perhaps they are already across the street from you, but they have decided to wake up and deliver the same level of service you are offering. That candle and cake idea is starting to fade fast in your mind. It's becoming a fistfight competition. But does it have to be that way? My response is no, but you must stop waving at your neighbors (customers).

Here are a few secrets to creating loyal neighbors. First, they will purchase from you even when someone offers a better price or is located five miles closer than you. You may be thinking that's not possible. You said earlier that no one could refuse an awesome deal. Well, it's time to level up with you; you and I can refuse a great buy.

Allow me to also apologize for not being honest with you. There's an even greater force that is driving our buying behavior. It's your heart.

The second secret, the heart, is responsible for our thinking, not our mind. You cannot go against what your heart feels. Before your heart allows you to go against it, it will cause you to be placed on medication or have a nervous breakdown.

So, how do you tap into the thinking part of the body?

Find ways to contribute to local community projects. Your neighbors will feel it in their hearts on what you are doing to support their communities. Remember, you must go beyond waving at your neighbors. That's equivalent to greeting your customers and asking if you can help them in the store.

Supporting local school projects is critical, from elementary schools to colleges and universities. It could mean helping to revitalize a community park or purchasing the uniform for a community softball team.

Support can be on a small scale, such as helping with the landscaping project of an older person in the community. Our older population is often the most forgotten members of our society.

Volunteering at a local soup kitchen has its rewards as well.

Understanding the diagnostics of human behavior is becoming more critical in terms of survival in business. There is a part two to this conversation: winning without fearing the competition or, better yet, annihilating the competition with ease.

I promised myself that I would not share that strategy in this book on making the competition irrelevant statistically. Well, allow me to give you a simple strategy of what I am referring to. The chronological path to human behavior is predictable, and you can shift it to your advantage. Our emotions are stronger than our IQ. Emotions generate feelings; feelings dictate your actions.

Perhaps you think we can place our brains on autopilot. Yes. But I'm not going to reveal that secret in this book. However, I will leave that strategy up to you and your team of leaders.

Knowledge can be deadly. Trust me, as I have been in a knowledge-based situation. Allow me to give you an example of how critical knowledge can be. If the propeller on your airplane stops at seven thousand feet in the air, your understanding of how to get that propeller back in rotation becomes life or death.

I challenge you to think of your business in that same vein. Also, get to know your neighbors on your turf via kids' workshops, customer clinics, women's night-out clinics, and contractor clinics. What they learn about you, and you learn about them, allows you to know your neighbors on a meaningful level.

Business is war without bloodshed; just because you don't see the blood does not mean you are not in conflict with the competition. Your leaders must understand their associates and customers on a scientific level. Just knowing the financials is not enough to drive the business forward. The laws of reciprocity are fundamental. Thus, helping members of your local community is beneficial to your organization.

# Chapter Three

# I Watched the Fish Die

If you have ever wondered what the parts of a business are, they are a company's heart, mind, and soul. Allow me to translate these parts into organizational parts. Like the organs that keep us alive, these parts keep a company alive. If you lose sight of these parts, your company can be placed on life support, just like when your organs fail.

Culture, people, and numbers are crucial components of a company. Your company culture is the heart of your organization, and depending on the size of your company, if you lose the culture, your company begins to die a slow death. It's vital to keep a pulse check on your culture. When you hire or promote an individual, your first thought should be—*can this person live by the culture of this company?* Also, do you see this person adding value to the company culture? If you have a slight doubt as to whether or not this person can be of supreme value to the company culture, I recommend you move on to the next candidate. It's just that vital.

Often, we hire or promote a person because we tell ourselves that the person is very smart, has a proven track record of delivering results, or has a degree in this field of work. I'm here to tell you none of that matters if they can't live by the company's culture. If you discover that you have made the wrong hire or promotion of an individual, it's okay; we all have made poor decisions in our careers as leaders. What's not okay is that you allow that person to continue working in their role for the organization. Doing so is not living by the company culture.

You can't allow yourself to see evidence of how a person is poorly performing in the culture category and not take action. Either you demote the individual or terminate them from the company; there is too much at stake for you to pay no heed to what everyone else knows.

We agreed that people are the second most crucial aspect of a company. This idea may seem extreme. You may wonder why you can't save him or her. Here's what you need to know about an organ transplant: the body will continue to try and reject the new body part. Your body knows this new body part is not a part of its original part. Trying to change the behavior of an individual who is wired a certain way is nearly impossible; their DNA will reject this new mind transplant. Therefore, you are wasting your time.

Having the right people in your company is like having an open vein in the body. Your people are the conduit for making things happen. Culture cannot exist without people. When the culture is right, you have a sustainable company; a strong culture gives you a 20 percent advantage over the competition.

If your competitor is struggling in this area, this is an opportune time for your company to double down on its values and culture. Doing so will increase your competitive advantage to an even wider gap.

The right people do matter. As Tom Peters famously said, "The brand is the talent."

Most leaders will tell you they just need to develop the right strategy, and they can win over the competition. Here's what you need to know about strategy, according to Peter Drucker—"culture eats strategy for breakfast every day."

Culture plays a paramount role in the sustainability of a company. I have heard people say that a misplaced, cultured leader is just one person in the company, and everything will be okay. Here's my reply to that statement, "polluted water affects every fish in the tank." As conscious leaders, we cannot stand by and watch the fish die.

We all know that numbers are indeed necessary for staying alive in business. However, I recommend you don't burn up all your free fuel on chasing metrics. Your financial results will be a byproduct of driving a substantial value-based culture.

Eighty-five percent of the CEOs agree that having a solid culture is their number one concern in their company. However, only 15 percent of the companies have a strong culture. Most companies have an effective counsel group, and they come up with some cool ideas and strategies that the company can implement company-wide. These individuals have also come up with some tremendous labor-saving programs. In addition, they are often the voice of your employees, bringing forth some insight into what the employees view as an issue or concern.

Let's change the narrative for a bit. What if your organization has a weak to no culture? If that's the case, then no sublime strategy can prevent your company from the inevitable; you will most likely become a victim of deception of the gradual. Some events and businesses are moving at a pace that is undetected by what we see or hear, and when that takes effect, failure can be a few feet away or just around the corner. However, an effective culture group can be the saving grace for an organization. Honestly speaking, only you know the true health culture of your company.

Remember, every employee, regardless of their position, from entry-level to senior position in the company, comes to work with three words on the top of their mind—*Do I Matter*? If this question is not resolved in their mindset, then there is no compelling reason for them to remain employed there. The great migration of resignation is real, and I can't repeat this statement enough. The values and culture of a company must be deeply rooted and alive and well within your company. Turnover of employees is costing companies millions of dollars each year. The sad reality is that you can mitigate most of this by inspecting your culture.

It's not the money or the opportunity for advancement that keeps your employees there. If you are in a position where people report to you, the question becomes, are you connecting with them on a meaningful level. If your response is yes, just make sure it's authentic. You can't fake being genuine. Your people will spot fake authentication a mile away. In addition, are you connecting with the community on a meaningful level as well? Don't forgo this opportunity to make a real difference in the communities around you.

Your customers are paying attention to the causes you support. In closing, ensure you are not funding another program or strategy within your organization unless you can say with 100 percent certainty that your values and the company culture are intact. You could save millions of dollars each year if you could hold on to the talented people you already have.

We often place many of our job openings on third-party sites. Can you guess who your biggest recruiters are to fill open positions within the company? If you guessed your current employees, you guessed it correctly. Everything seems to fall in line with a positive associate relations environment.

# Chapter Four

# I'm Dealing with Blue Flames

Every supervisor or leader enjoys their new promotion. What an exciting time hearing the words, "Congratulations on your promotion." For certain, I can reflect on when I was promoted; those words are forever etched into my memory. You go from managing yourself to managing others. I can also recall when I stopped clocking in as an associate; I kept stopping by the time clock for the first thirty days. It's amazing how our mind operates. Clearly, I knew I had been promoted; it was just a force of habit that kept me stopping by that time clock.

It also felt different when giving directions to others. Stepping into another level of paperwork shifts the mind as well. You also start addressing some of the associates' and customers' concerns. The first few concerns or problems get resolved relatively easily. You start thinking that you should have applied for the position long ago. I can't believe how well this is going for me.

For the first few months, the associates and leaders around you ask if there is anything they can do for you. Your mind takes on another mental shift: why isn't everyone going for a promotion? It comes with more pay and a higher status. The first six months of a promotion is always the most exciting time of your role. People are prone to tell you how great you are.

We have been conditioned to the stories we have heard as kids. They relaxed us and even helped us fall asleep at night. So, if someone tells us a fiction story, it's okay. We still feel good about it. You approach the one-year mark in position your position, and the first layer of varnish has worn off. The congratulations are over, and the expectations have set in. The metrics are not trending in the direction you want them to go. In addition, the leaders below you are not moving at the speed you need them to. You anticipate feeling some heat, with the understanding that you are expected to be able to perform in your role. Anyone can deal with some heat, but what happens when the fire turns red to blue flames?

Here's what you need to know about fire: when all flame colors combine, the color is white-blue, which is the hottest. Also, nothing remains the same when fire touches it. It shapes and molds whatever it touches. When leaders feel the pressure, it shapes and molds who they are, for the good or bad. You will inevitably be changed. With that, your title as a leader cannot overshadow your discomfort due to stress.

You may be surprised to know the number of leaders who have achieved public success but endured private failure. Allow me to also go on record by saying that being an effective leader is getting more challenging as the speed of disruption increases daily. Your style of managing others changes when the fire has gone from red to blue.

A new leader will not understand the significance of their words. They will often confuse intent with impact. Most leaders have great intentions but have a harmful effect on others. Even steel is shaped by fire, so what makes us think human behavior will not be shaped by fire? The question becomes, are we better under pressure?

Most inexperienced leaders without tenure think they are dealing with blue flames. It would be great to see a company develop a blue flame program. What would that program look like?

You will be appointed an executive coach depending on your position level with the company. If your leadership position is lower in rank, you will be assigned a mentor; this mentor must check in with you monthly. An experienced person in your same role can be of extreme help. More than likely, they have been through many blue flame moments and have survived those blue flame encounters successfully.

In my early flying days, I encountered a blue flame moment in the air, and the single propeller on our plane stopped. I was thankful to have been with an experienced blue-flame co-pilot that day. I don't think I could have written this book if it had not been for him.

I was trying to reflect on my training when the propeller stopped. Doing this is where muscle memory should have kicked in, but let me tell you, it is hard to think when you are in crisis mode. My mind had already shifted from step one, trying to get the propeller back in rotation, to step two, looking for an open field or clear road to land the plane.

When leaders are under blue flames, they often create an environment where team members are watching their backs versus having each other's backs. There is so much momentum lost from individuals working solo. This is highly visible in spots. A great football coach said it best, "team beats talent when talent is not a team." When a leader fails, the common theme among upper leaders is that they didn't see it coming. No one sees the potential train wreck coming. Why? Because most leaders have too much pride to seek counsel, they suffer in silence. However, if the company had a blue flame program, it could have saved that leader from demotion or termination.

When a leader is in crisis mode, they shift into the mindset of thinking they will get rid of everyone before they go. That is clearly not an effective survival method, but it would be the same as trying to step out of an airplane while it descends.

I intentionally didn't outline all of the details of a blue-flame program in this chapter because every company is different and will need to tailor a program to its unique circumstances. In addition, depending on the layers of leadership positions, each tier must be customized to support that leader. If you are a new leader or thinking about becoming one, I recommend seeking self-improvement programs. Committing to reading as often as possible will give you a huge advantage. Or go out on your own and hire an executive coach. I have hired a few in my career journey, which has yielded dividends ten times over. Frequently, the cavalry will not show up on time, and you must give yourself every advantage when leading and managing through one of the most challenging eras of business.

The pandemic has changed us as a society in many ways. Patience, empathy, humbleness, and appreciation are the most common decency human attributes that have evaporated. We have interred into a microwave society. Everything is urgent, and companies and leaders are expected to deliver at a high level every quarter. With this knowledge, I recommend "you brew you," meaning start investing in yourself today; don't wait on a company program to help you become better as a leader. Seek out others you trust, ask for their recommendation on finding a great business coach, or there are some great online courses. Whatever helps you get the percolation going this week. Saying you did not know is not a viable excuse today.

Me saying I didn't know the propeller would stop—telling someone of my crisis while in the air—would not have done me a bit of good. I needed to launch into action to make it home to my family that day. Just because you are on the ground, you are flying, but no one has told you. So, avoid thinking you have time to improve yourself.

# Chapter Five

# I Did Not Choose Leadership

Being in a leadership position can be one of the most rewarding positions an individual could land. You are afforded the opportunity to transform the environment you represent. Yes, some complexities come along with the role. Working and enduring long hours is one of them. Also, there is pressure to deliver profitability while leveraging controllable expenses. The expectation for meeting all of your metrics is becoming increasingly critical. Even with all of those mentioned above, being in a leadership role is, in my opinion, a dream job.

So, what makes it hard?

Many people want to *be* leaders but do not want to *do* leadership. Yes, there is a difference between the two. You may be still thinking, what about leadership makes it so complex? If the answer did not jump off the page on you, dealing with people makes it complex. Hold on to that mental statement before you say, *I knew it,* and follow me on this mental journey.

As a young boy, I was a part of the Boys and Girls Club. I remember one of the volunteers there purchasing a pair of shoes for a young boy who showed up weekly with holes in his shoes. While in high school, I recall one of my teachers showing my male classmate how to tie his necktie as he was going for a job interview the following week. This classmate did not have a male role model at home. I also recall a man in my neighborhood purchasing a bike for a young girl whose parents could not afford to buy her one when all of the other kids had one in the neighborhood. As a young man, I could not forget those words that everyone used to say about someone who expressed a deep concern for the welfare of others.

These were folklore terms. However, the words will never leave me. When you would see this person in public, the one responsible for those great deeds, we used to say, "Momma, that's him; he's the one that bought that bike for Cassandra." "Momma, that's him; he's the one that bought those shoes for James." "Momma, that's him; he's the one who taught Charles how to tie his necktie for his job interview."

Those adults were performing from the heart. Therefore, those deeds were not complex tasks. If you say you did not choose leadership, leadership chose me, then you have accepted the responsibility of being a leader.

The workplace should be a conducive environment where everyone cohabitates.

What will be your legacy when you move on? Perhaps one day, before you leave that role, someone will see you in public and say, "Momma, that's him; he's the manager who asks everyone how their family is doing." "Momma, that's him; he's the manager that visited Sam, my co-worker at the hospital." "Momma, that's him; he's the leader that made sure Jim could make it to his son's college graduation five hours away when my co-worker Jim had already exhausted all of his paid time off." "That's him, Momma!"

What will be your legacy?

My mother was a single parent when I was between five and seven. When we were out in public, it was a training day. She took advantage of this opportunity to train me on the fundamentals of how to treat people—when to say please, thank you, and you're welcome. More importantly, she would tell me, "Son, people will forget many words you tell them in life, but no one will forget how you made them feel. Make sure you treat everyone with respect. Remember, you will always be doing better than some but worse than others. And never look down on someone that has less than you."

After leaving home, I went on to achieve a four-year degree. Yes, I ascertained some great knowledge and acquired some very needed discipline. I also know of many who went on to some great Ivy League universities for their graduate degree(s), and all of those schools were excellent universities. Somewhere along the way, you will most likely receive training on diversity, inclusion, and bias views you may be harboring unbeknownst to yourself. When or if you have already received this training, I think you will concur, the training is excellent.

While writing this book, I picked up the phone and called my mother. I thanked my mom for teaching me everything I needed about diversity, inclusion, bias, and unbiased views. She was able to achieve this while I was a young boy.

People are not the job's complexity, but rather the failed training at a young age. I received my "Momma, that's him" moment a few times in my leadership career. Understanding people is to love people. Thank You, Mom!

Every institution, regardless of its size, needs to work toward creating a productive cultural environment for all. It can't be a glorious contextualization we talk about; we need to practice it.

What does practice look like, connecting with people where they are? I am more concerned with a multi-contextual environment than a multicultural space. Collective thinking can bring forth a sublime platform of purity.

# Chapter Six

# Running at My Own Speed

There is tremendous pleasure in being in control. It gives us a sense of accomplishment and enjoyment. We have been conditioned to this feeling from a very young age. For example, which outfit would you like to wear today, the blue or the green shirt? You were nudged on moving forward on the low end of what was taking place. On the high end, choice architecture was being enacted on you. This term, coined by Thaler and Sunstein, refers to the practice of influencing choice by organizing the context in which people make decisions.

My mother raised seven kids as a single parent. With that said, she operated on the other side of choice architecture—*wear this or else*. I can assure you, wearing *this* was a better choice.

In business, as individual contributors or leaders, we make choices based on many internal and external factors. No decision is made as a sole contributor. The question becomes where and what is influencing our choices.

Let me move you a little further down the path; many of our choices are on autopilot. The illusion of control has given many of us a state of contentment. Advertisers know this choice architecture algorithm far too well. Making sound decisions can be very complex; your thoughts move just behind the speed of light, which is 10 seconds. We are running at our own speed when we make a choice.

Speed can be beneficial when it comes to the fight-or-flight responses. Your life may depend on it. However, sometimes, we have made an impulse decision that yields a negative output. There are no mental slow-down or speed-up signs in the brain. We are allowed to travel mentally at our own speed. With that speed of mental free will, you can easily engage in catastrophic behavior.

If you hire an executive coach to help strengthen your leadership skills, ensure they are fluent in understanding culture and identity. Here's why: the human brain is in constant duality between how we see ourselves and others. When the mind is in duality, this can result in confusion in terms of identity and self-esteem. If our negative emotions go unresolved, what someone says or does can trigger our emotions at any time. They become consistent fuel to our confusion as our brains will keep trying to justify why we behave irrationally. Understanding the foundational mechanism of the brain allows us to become self-aware and can significantly enrich our moral compass in leadership.

Allow me to take it one step further to explain why I feel coaching is critical and necessary at all levels of leadership. Here's an unknown fact: if we are confronted with differences in opinion, the chemicals released in the brain are the same ones that try to ensure survival in dangerous situations.

Let's bring it down one layer and describe it in layperson's terms. You may have witnessed individuals at picnic gatherings, concerts, or sports games get into fights after spending perhaps hours celebrating together. In this situation, someone disagrees with another person or the group. A chemical had been released in the brain unbeknownst to both parties, which provoked the fight-or-flight response in the brain.

As leaders, we may not engage in fight-or-flight responses. However, we may not guard our words or actions when someone confronts us with a difference of opinion in a lower role. Yes, the same chemical is being released in your brain; there are no exceptions. So, you may think about how to avoid or overcome this chemical response controlling your actions.

Understanding the chronological path to human behavior is one way. There is a much deeper mental process that you must engage in to equip yourself better when confronted by this chemical. The second way is to know that emotions are stronger than IQ. You must learn to overcome self. There is a process for this as well.

Before I discovered the chronological path to action, I was also acting on my emotions. I spent many years with a top executive coach who put me through a series of mental training, such as contemplating quantum physics and string theory. One of the key points that my executive coach made sure he landed with me was understanding that when we are self-aware, we can alter our misplaced emotions because we control the thoughts that cause them. This concept had a profound effect on my leadership behavior. He also stressed that we should always suspend judgments and gather facts first. As leaders, we often rush to judgment without considering the facts. Remember, there are no stop or slow-down signs in the brain. Your brain, if left untrained, can work for or against you. I acquired incredible control over my feelings after learning and practicing these concepts.

Most of our thoughts and actions are impulsive when we are unaware. Don't allow yourself to be divorced from proper training. You are too important to the company brand you represent. Reading this book is an investment in your leadership growth—the maturing leadership process. If we stay on the right course of mentorship, there will be nothing we can't ultimately accomplish. When we go it alone, we limit the positive impact coaching can have.

Don't try to tiptoe your way through leading others; your team deserves more. Be an effective leader that people desire to replicate. Make sure the people you lead know that you appreciate them. People are becoming more distant from their companies because they believe their work is not appreciated. Why not be alkaline in their water and raise the pH in their attitude by caring?

The element of choice is real: retain your people by being the place people want to work because of your leadership. Turnover of employees is an expensive proposition for all companies. However, you can curve that loss by being a conscious leader.

# Chapter Seven

# Seemingly Logical Attribute

I believe in getting directly to the point. With that being said, don't take everything so personally. I have spoken to many individuals throughout my career as a leader. And many of the stories I hear are exaggerated. People are generally indifferent to your fate, not as antagonistic as you imagine. Very few of their actions are rarely directed at you. Stop seeing everything in personal terms. Respect must be earned through your achievements, not something given to you simply for being human. Yes, you will experience some adversity in the workplace. If I have not said it, this would be a perfect time to make this statement: life is 10 percent what happens to you and 90 percent how you respond. You are always in control. Never go through life trying to avoid any kind of adversity. First of all, it's very tedious to live a life without challenges.

Here's how to avoid disappointment: take a realistic assessment of yourself and your limits. It may also come as a surprise, but envy may be the root of your disappointment in others. Many of us suffer from a delusion of success and are unaware of its effects on our mindset.

I have witnessed many people go through a string of promotions. They were in the right place at the right time. Yes, the timing was a factor. It's often said that high tide raises all ships. With that metaphor, their ship rose to the top.

There should be a bit of caution that comes along with rapid promotions. Have you heard of the term " fooled by randomness?" We often experience a high level of achievement and reach significant milestones on a task or metric, and it's usually due to the collaboration of the team contribution. This is where we should be pumping the breaks and reassessing ourselves. Well, that's not always the case. Far too often, the mind tells us we are the sole contributor to our success. In a more reckless mindset, we believe we are the genius and everyone else is a dummy. It will happen to the best of us; the further you go up the corporate ladder, the more you feel you were much better at it in your prior role.

You must seek out ways to remain humble and grounded. Remember, you are among many in the world and not naturally superior to anyone. You are not a god or an angel but a flawed human like the rest of us. You must accept that you cannot control the people around you and that no strategy is foolproof. Human nature is too unpredictable. As Fannie Lou Hamer so elegantly stated, "The examined life is painful." It takes courage to examine who you are.

Another way to stay grounded is to consider developing a new skill in an unrelated field or writing a book. This is a good distraction from the real work. You will lose valuable character dimensions when you forget who you are.

Our thinking and ways of acting become rigid. Here's the great news: you will fascinate people by being authentically yourself. The one thing you can't do is live with a Peter Pan complex, which is never to grow up. At some point, you must mature and grow up. A key element to growing up is to take responsibility for your actions. As a leader of people, you have a tremendous responsibility to nurture, coach, and inspire others. However, to indulge in any of these activities, you must develop the skill set of being humane.

In addition, you need to have an endless appetite for all aspects of life and a deep admiration for the welfare of others. You can take on another approach. However, I can assure you it is short-lived. Being moody, self-absorbed, and high-strung is not a lasting leadership attribute. Yes, your position will be in jeopardy. Know that there is a thin line between asset and liability, and you can go from asset to liability within twenty-four hours, based on your words or actions.

Allow me to give you this tell of caution. In my adolescent years, I used the word *adolescent* to excuse myself for my actions, although I was old enough to know better. I was seeking to advance myself on the job. However, the advancement was not happening fast enough, in my view. So, what did I do next? I allowed my emotions to take the front seat. Once my emotions were in the driver's seat, I began seeking advice from others on what to do. The advice I received from others went from the sublime to the ridiculous.

Coming to terms with this understanding is invaluable. Know that advice is free, and believe me when I tell you, people will give you a lot of free advice, a liberal dose of advice. Why? Because your actions come at no cost to them.

Here's what happened in my case. I was working very hard to advance myself in my career path. Being young, I took the ridiculous advice because it made great sense to me then. I walked up to my manager, told him I quit, gave him my apron, and walked out. I felt great walking away and leaving the job. However, once I got home, I started reflecting on how stupid my decision was, not knowing how I would pay my bills. I also began reflecting on all of that free advice that I was getting, especially from the one person who told me to quit and walk out—that would show them how much they would miss a great associate.

Within five hours of quitting, I became a genius in common sense. I called the store manager and got my job back. What a valuable lesson I learned on getting free advice. I shared my experience to say anyone can give advice, but not everyone is suitable. Be very selective about who you are digesting advice from. It's okay to listen, and often you can't avoid it. But don't take it in.

I was fortunate to be able to get my job back. When I told him I quit, my store manager did not process my termination. However, I had two attributes in my favor. First, I never called out sick. Also, I told management that whenever someone called out sick to call me, I was always willing to take their hours and mine. Second, I ensured my output was always greater than anyone else in the store. When closing down a department, I would be the first one to get my department closed down, cleaned, and ready for the next day's business. Once my department was done, I would go seek out a manager to see who else needed help closing down their department.

Management would love to close with me. Word got around that I would close down my department plus two to three other departments. I had a plan the minute I clocked in to start the closing process while helping customers. My strategy was to prepare my department for closing two to three hours earlier. As soon as the front door was closed, I ran to get a manager. My first response to the manager was to ask who needed help in their department. The manager would often ask if I was already done. My reply was always to check my department. Also, it was a part of my daily mission to have a customer seek out a manager and rave about my customer service skills. If you were a customer and came into contact with me, you would receive the gold-star treatment.

As you read this chapter, I'm unsure where you are in your career. However, I encourage you to be the best you can be.

# Chapter Eight

# What Gift is in the Box?

There are a lot of emotions we exude with the exchange of a gift. When you were a kid, I'm sure when you received a gift on your birthday or a special occasion, it was memorable. Just having someone hand you a gift bag or box can release chemicals of joy, or knowing that you received a gift at a later time frame sets your mind in ecstasy. We will perform a task with a high sense of urgency if we know there will be a form of a gift after completing that task. Often, we use a gift to motivate people toward a mission.

When you set a goal for yourself, you often reward yourself with a gift after achieving that goal. It can appear that we live our lives based on feelings and emotions. Before you say it can't be true, some people can't go twenty-four hours without a compliment. If they don't receive a form of praise or recognition within twenty-four hours, they will set the stage to receive one or the other. They will post something on social media for someone to acknowledge. Then, check their phone or computer every half hour to see if someone responded to their post. If that doesn't work, they will likely move into phase two, call a close friend, and guilt them into responding to their post.

With the above said, we're on a vertical regarding people seeking positive recognition. As a leader equipped with this knowledge, you can make a huge difference in the environment you lead.

I believe we, as leaders, can shorten the distance between fact and fiction between our subordinates and employees. Yes, even with all of the great deeds a company may be doing for its employees, you will still have a small percentage of employees telling themselves the wrong story. The employees will often believe that no one acknowledges them for their outstanding work, or they wonder why the company can't do this or that for them. In fact, their company could be first-class in terms of what they do for their employees compared to other companies. As a leader, you can be the gap closer to creating the right environment along with what your company is already doing for its employees.

As a disclaimer, amnesia of good deeds did not vaporize during the pandemic. Pre-pandemic, there were still those out there wanting more and more of their company or forgetting about all the tangible monetary and nonmonetary contributions their company has given to its employees and their surrounding communities.

There is no statistical data backing what I'm about to say to you. I just wanted to go on record before making this statement. Being in a leadership role today is far more complex than being an attorney, doctor, or dentist. For example, an attorney knows the law and most amateurs will not tangle with them. If you decide to engage an attorney, you run the risk of looking foolish fast. That's the purpose of hiring your own attorney. In addition, there are consequences for not following the counsel of your paid attorney.

Another example is that a doctor's lab coat already puts them in an authoritative position. Anyone with good sense (pun intended) will not tell their doctor; they will perform their own brain operation.

At this point, you may think you can't solicit or command that type of leadership respect from your employees. However, before you relinquish the importance of your leadership title, follow me on this compelling yet necessary path. Amid distress, people yearn for hope and thirst for consciousness that only a leader can give them. With that said, not all managers are leaders. So, how do we delineate one from the other?

Many managers will tell you they were passionate about getting their position, even dedicated to going after their promotion. You can be committed and passionate about something but not gifted in that arena. The question is, can a person survive at something they are not gifted in? The answer is yes, but passion for something is not enough if you are not gifted in it.

Here's what you need to know about passion. A passion is what you love to do, but a gift is what you are born to do. You can thrive at something, even if you lose your passion, due to your gift. You see, your gift is not a talent. If it were, you could turn it on and off when you choose. Your gift makes you feel obligated.

Allow me to let you in on another secret hidden in plain sight. The entire logic of your life is hidden within your gift. Therefore, you must ask yourself if you are doing something you are gifted at because living a life of misery can be avoided. I made this statement in a prior chapter. However, it's worth repeating. Anyone who has achieved public success because of their title but endures private failure because they have engaged in something that is not their gift is bordering on the catastrophic.

You may even tell me you love what you do, but again, it's not enough. You can thrive and even amass a great degree of wealth, but the question is, are you happy?

I discovered my gift early on in life. I have the ability to connect with people on a meaningful level, which led me to lead others. My gift is a byproduct of being in a leadership role. I tried walking away from connecting with others many times in my life. However, my gift led me back into a leadership role.

Tupac Shakur made this profound statement in one of his songs, "I didn't choose rapping; rapping chose me." Perhaps he was on to something. If you find yourself in a job or position that you are successful in but can't seem to get into another profession, even if you have been trying for some time, maybe you didn't choose that profession; it chose you. This choice or chosen profession could even be in a non-profit organization or volunteering your time to a cause.

I close with this: Have you asked yourself if what you're currently doing is your gift in life? If you find it hard to answer that question, it's time to unite with your heart. The brain often lies to you, but the heart can never lie. Listen to your heart; yes, it will speak to you.

# Chapter Nine

# Are You Giving Out C.A.S.H Today

I have spent over three decades in retail and know what it feels like to get paid, but not in the monetary form you may think of. Yes, many people enjoy getting paid in exchange for performing a task or job. However, contrary to popular belief, cash is not king, but caring about someone honestly is.

Reflecting on my early years in retail, I thank God someone honestly cared about me. I hated to admit this in my early twenties, but I was lost, discouraged, and confused. However, because somebody cared enough about me, it changed my direction. I entered retail as an invisible individual; at least, that's how I felt.

Being a truth teller, you must be willing to admit your shortcomings. A leadership mind can no longer focus solely on the financials. That is not to say we do not have a fiduciary responsibility as a leader. If you work for a company that is a for-profit business, that must be at the top of your mind every second of the day. However, compartmentalizing your priorities is critical. Your people need a leader who knows how to drive the business but is compassionate at the same time.

I estimate that leaders who possess the skills of creating versus draining energy while maintaining a positive employee relations environment will be in short supply. Common decency skills in business are fading fast, and in many cases, it is a lost art. Many may ask why this is happening and why so many leaders have lost this art. It's very simple—pressure.

When under pressure, we think IQ is the answer, only to find that EQ is the solution. You can't learn how to deal with a crisis while in a crisis. Yet, we tell leaders to learn that skill every day.

The best remedy is to pressure test your business or operations while things are going great. Come up with a few worst-case scenarios for your operations. For example, what if you lose 25-30 percent of your business or your transactions drop by 25 percent? What if your average ticket is down 7 percent compared to the prior year? In addition, your inventory of your top products is low, and you can't get the items any time soon.

You can go with the quick fix that everyone goes to and cut payroll by X percent, or you can give your team members permission to think freely. Some of the greatest ideas have been born from being in a crisis, and not all great ideas come from a corporate office.

You may wonder how we can achieve this during a pandemic. I ask you to consider that the pandemic is only alive for those who see it. Others see the opportunity to drive sales, average tickets, attach rate, and increase margin while creating better customer relationships. However, none of this can happen if leaders have their hands around employees' throats. You throttle your team with meetings and conference calls for every metric you miss. Perhaps you should immediately pressure test team calls or meetings.

If you don't believe this could help your business in a crisis, research the many businesses born during a crisis that became mega businesses.

The chapter title is more than a heading; it's the foundation for retaining and nurturing great talent.

No matter how great new leaders are, the erosion of rejection will start bombarding their minds at some point. Most talented leaders are trying to get the information by themselves without the benefit of a mentor or any sponsorship or tutelage. My hope is that you take heed to this early edition of what's to come in the minds of many. You often hear the word *blindsided* in business, but did you really get caught off guard, or just did you ignore the subtle signs of the future state?

The human mindset is shifting in ways that many fail to understand. The behavior of individuals is more complex than playing chess. At least in a chess game, your opponent taps the bell to let you know that they have made a move and it's your turn. But what if you could shape the decision of your opponent or the new leader before they decide their next move? Well, you can if you understand the mechanics of choice architecture. I spoke about this in an earlier chapter. The question becomes whether you know enough about the human psyche or are running your operations or business from a myopic perspective.

For myself, I am never concerned with someone's present state of thinking, but I am very interested in the velocity and depth of someone's thinking. It's a great indicator of their predictable actions, and it also uncovers their past exposure and how they will respond to certain situations.

The flow of time is so embedded in who we are. It is my hypothesis that if you can determine where a thought is derived from, you can then shape the person's actions.

Our reasoning skills are divided into two parts: systematic and logical or unconscious and emotional. However, velocity, depth, and time play a huge role in our governing factors for decision making.

We can also view time as experience.

You can delineate an individual thought pattern by digesting what I shared in this chapter. Remember, we are pattern-driven human beings. I just gave you surface-level training on becoming a choice designer. You can influence people's choices; emotions are stronger than IQ.

Provided I was given enough face time with you, I can place your brain on autopilot. You will only be in control by thought but not by actions. I leave you with this thought-provoking question: do you have permission to make choices for yourself, or have your choices been made for you days, months, or years in advance?

If you say: I follow you but don't get you. Or, if all the dots don't connect, you should hire a mentor or coach. The simple fact is you can't change what you don't understand.

# Chapter Ten

# I Don't Get in The Water

The upside of working in retail is that it has tremendous benefits. You can start your career in a lower entry-level position and work up to a desired role. The ladder goes straight up if you choose to advance yourself in your company.

Reflecting on my entry-level position, I was hired to clean the restrooms and collect shopping carts in the parking lot at $4.25 an hour. While in orientation, the store manager facilitating the onboarding stated to everyone in orientation that they would have the opportunity to learn and grow their career with the company. He shared with the group that he started his career as an associate in the garden department before becoming a store manager. He also declared that many of us would become district managers and even regional vice presidents. He spoke those words as if he was given special permission to look into the future.

Well, I went on to become a district manager.

There is something special about speaking with conviction. It has a powerful effect on our belief about what we can or cannot ascertain in life. The power of influence is embedded in what we give credence to.

Please allow me to give you a piece of sage advice: if you don't plan on growing your career and moving into a higher role, it is perfectly fine, talent is required at every level. Therefore, you are appreciated and needed even if those words are not spoken to you directly. However, I will caution you that our mind is our greatest gift and enemy. You must look for ways to keep yourself inspired. Far too often, we place that burden on a supervisor or manager. They will most likely have plenty on their plate.

Before you make a mental commitment here, that's not to say your supervisor has the right to talk down to you or belittle you. What I am saying is, don't give someone that type of autonomy over your happiness; there is greatness within you. But that greatness can be lit or put out by the story you tell yourself. Believe me when I tell you this; I am speaking from experience.

Overcoming myself was my biggest hurdle. I was in constant pursuit of external validation. In my inexperienced years as an associate and supervisor, I was easily distracted by a lack of praise. The mind algorithm for next-level leadership is something I had to learn from an executive coach. I decided to end the error of pretending I had it all together. Coaching was life-changing for me. My executive coach was able to undo the mental damage I had done to myself as well as the damage I had allowed my co-workers to do. I also discovered from my coach that I preferred to feel rather than think.

Guess what, I don't think I was alone. In fact, I believe many people are living this way today. We are motivated by what people say and think about us. We tend to rely on weak-minded individuals for our support and drive to perform.

In America, there are 3,500 accidental drownings each year, which means there are ten drownings a day. It's not due to a lack of knowledge; as we know, access to learning how to swim is all around us. But whether or not we take advantage of the learning within reach.

Here's what's more shocking: a weak swimmer can't save a drowning victim. If a weak swimmer tries to save a drowning person, more than likely, both will drown because the skill or strength is not there. So, the question becomes, why are you tied to a trifling person on the job who doesn't have the strength to pull you up? I have witnessed many careers die due to someone else's ignorance. With that said, I don't get in the water. Linking up with negative people on the job is equivalent to having an untrained swimmer trying to save you from drowning. I am not new to this, but true to this.

Here's my drowning story. I was hanging with many non-swimmers at work, and they convinced me to jump in the proverbial deep water at work. The problem was I did not know how to swim. I took their advice and told the manager I quit and walked out with no job lined up or plans on how I would pay my bills. Yes, I was in the water without swimming lessons. I understand this may have been a graphic depiction explaining my point. However, I am willing to do whatever it takes to save the careers of the potential victims who listen to the wrong or ill-intent co-workers.

What good is it to underscore the problem without providing you with a solution? Acquiring a mentor or executive coach can be life-changing for you. The lessons will amaze you. In addition, you will most likely experience a quantum leap in your understanding of human behavior and gain the leadership foresight that is needed in the 21st century.

We have never seen the volatility, complexity, and transformation we see today. Things are exponentially accelerating in business at a speed that most leaders are unprepared to deal with. This progress has changed the landscape of work, education, and our lives. Today, leaders are given a deck of cards they don't understand or cannot grasp, and they cannot grasp the nature and impact of the hand they have been dealt. Holding on with the white knuckle effect and waiting for the ride to slow down or stop will likely not happen.

Allow me to share the words of my executive coach, "Don't wish for things to get easier, but channel your energy on getting better." If you say you can't afford to hire an executive coach, make sure you know how to get to your nearest library or bookstore. Remember, it's not a lack of access to knowledge but our inability to engage in what is at our disposal.

It may be hard to conceptualize and digest what I share with you. However, you must think SELF first. Get off the opinion lifestyle and be true to yourself; you deserve it. You must try to avoid awakening one day only to find out you regret your choices based on someone else's viewpoint.

I can assure you there are no refunds for regrets in life. We must live with the decisions we have made and then move on. You can and will persevere if you believe you can. Have I made all of the right decisions? Absolutely not. However, I never pretend to be a perfect leader. We are all flawed in some way. In fact, my pajamas don't match. So don't expect to receive any holiday pictures of me and my family with matching pajamas.

Speaking of transparency, I don't always wear the same socks, I often wear a blue and black sock. My point is to be willing to adjust and learn what will help you sustain yourself as a legendary leader. The probability of you running into a unicorn is more common than being led by an authentic leader. But you—yes, you—can be that authentic leader.

# Chapter Eleven

# The Joy of Spinning Wheels

In my early adult years, I owned my first three on-the-floor manual shift cars; what a joy this car was. I will go out on a limb and trust that my mom doesn't read this part of my book because she thought I was a very responsible young man and stayed out of trouble. For the most part, I did. However, I had my moments.

A group of friends and I would go to a grocery store parking lot after closing hours and do burnouts and donuts with our cars looking for that cloud of smoke from our tires. We would also find an open road to drag race. Doing burnouts was the highlight of our nights. I think our seeking smoke from our tires started before owning a car. We would ride our bicycles as fast as we could and then hit the back brakes and slide as long as we could, looking for a glimmer of smoke from our bicycle tires. On a good note, I grew out of these mischievous behaviors before I could cause any real damage to myself or my mother's reputation.

Back then, when I was growing up, it meant something to not trash your family's last name. If someone would witness you doing something wrong in the neighborhood, they would say, "That's Claudette's son. He's a Jones. He knows better than that. She is good people and raised her kids well."

The person who witnessed the poor behavior would take it a step further. They would say, "Come over here."

When you stepped over, they would say, "I know your mother personally, and this is not how she raised you."

That conversation alone would be enough to put you back on the right path of doing good versus wrong. I could carry that, making my mother proud of me throughout my career. In addition, I did not want anyone to look down on my mother because of my actions. I wanted her to be able to hold her head up high and be proud that I was her son.

What if someone told you they knew where you worked because of how you greeted them? They knew that only people from XYZ company showed that type of care for the welfare of others. What if everyone who worked for your company cared about their company's reputation outside of work? How would that change the world we live in? What if everyone in your company wanted their community to be proud of where you worked? What if a company was proud of you based on your deeds in the community? What if your community or company recognized you for making a real difference in the community?

Allow me to get a bit more serious here. I spoke about burnouts being a highlight for me in my youth. Well, experiencing burnout as an adult is not a pleasant moment for anyone. We, as leaders, must remain hyper-vigilant for those on the job who may be on the verge of going through burnout. You should be able to spot a behavior change or subtle sign if a worker is not being their usual self. No different from my childhood neighbors knowing when I was out of character. The critical factor in this equation is that the community engaged with me instead of pretending nothing was wrong with me. They knew when I was performing differently or not at my best potential.

What if we decided to become different leaders? What if you treated your associates as if they bore your last name?

My point is leaders should operate on a set of standards. However, most look at the crisis they are leading through as defeat. Here's what I know for sure: having low self-standards will place you at a disadvantage. I have noticed that this single action is by far the number one contributing factor to subpar performance, causing many leaders to perform below standards.

Measuring yourself by yourself is not wise. However, leaders are currently engaging in this tactic and believing that it's yielding a great return to themself. This behavior during the pandemic has led many leaders to think they are doing the right thing. When running a business during a crisis, you must focus on the defects regardless of size and scope. Remember your margins and turns, along with controlling your expenses, will most likely become life support for your business during a crisis. If you have a less tenured leader in place without proper mentorship, they could be spinning their wheels, and spinning wheels as an adult is not a good thing in business. What you need is traction.

Momentum is mission-critical in business. If I were your personal coach, we would first focus on helping you program your brain to be a limitless leader. Second, we would work on igniting your passion for the business after burnout. Believe me, you will experience burnout at some point in your career. It's okay as long as you know how to reignite your passion.

One of the things they teach you in flight training is how to get your propeller back in rotation after your engine stalls out in the air. Without the proper training, I think you already know the probability of landing safely.

Third, I would redirect your mind to the story you are telling yourself. You will, without a doubt, be operating at another frequency; there is no other way to explain it.

As long as you are growing as a leader, don't be as concerned with the speed of your growth. You just need momentum in your life.

If you find yourself standing still with little to no mental growth, try learning another language; this, by far, is one of the fastest ways to take your mind to the gym.

Unbeknownst to you, we are in a war for our thinking brains. I believe Dr. Joseph McFarland when he said, "Only 2 percent of the population thinks, 3 percent thinks they think, and 95 percent would rather die than think." I get it; it's far easier to live a life of repetition than to engage in thinking. You owe it to yourself to step away from just responding and engage in thinking.

A degree of thinking requires you to suspend judgment and gather the facts. Even the things you see and hear should be questioned. In addition, you must empty your mind of all thoughts to make clear decisions. We are not always making clear choices due to interrupted thoughts.

I must warn you decontaminating your mind is not easy. It takes practice and a great deal of training and focus. Most people will say they think every day. Not true; most people are responding and telling themselves they are thinking.

The heart of thinking requires you to care about your actions while suspending judgment with a level of conscious forethought. That's the true definition of conscious *being*. Why are you leading if your quest is not to arrive at this point? Do you care enough to battle, understand, or challenge yourself?

We spend a lot of our mental time in the wrong areas. More provoking questions are: What are you spending your time on? What are you spending your time doing? What are you paying attention to? That's where you will find real value.

I spent a great deal of my time in my early years of leadership on non-sense. What is at the end of this acquired knowledge is FREEDOM.

Good luck if you think you can walk away from this chapter and not make a conscious change. Your mind will resurface this content and remind you of the change you should have made when you discovered the information to do so but failed to engage.

It gets even more profound. Don't try and put consciousness in a box; you will fail. This may surprise you, even if you disagree with what I have shared with you, plus you have willfully decided to disregard this knowledge.

What's going on unbeknownst to you is something is already taking place inside you without your permission; your cells know when they discover truth. You are not the ruler of self, but your cells are.

You will experience chaos if you don't act on this knowledge. Chaos happens when there is imbalance and ignorance of truth. It is impossible to dumb your mind down once it has been exposed to the truth. You have no choice but to take action on it. I have witnessed someone go through a nervous breakdown, battling with their mind. We are wired and programmed to know when something is not right. It takes a conscious will to override this built-in factor. You must begin to love and appreciate the gifts that come with your body.

You were built perfectly before having your mind contaminated. It's time to treat yourself and others with respect and appreciation. Don't make any changes because of what I have said or shared with you. From this point forward, you are battling with self. Your internal mechanism is very powerful. Learn to flow with it, not against it. Do what's right by others and enjoy the fruits of your labor. Lead from the front, not from behind.

# Chapter Twelve

# Counterfeit Feelings

As a leader today, I'm sure you have already figured out that managing other's feelings has just become one of your key priorities in the workplace.

Many associates are becoming misguided with false impressions. What they often see and hear does not need to have any real truth to it; as long as it feels right to them, it's right. Yes, that's a dangerous way to live. But it's the reality they're living in. This interpretation of reality is gaining traction.

As you already know, your feelings can defraud you. In addition, when someone is caught up in their feelings, it is almost impossible to reason with them. Facts don't matter at that point. Even having a straightforward conversation with someone can be draining and challenging. Why? They often focus on how something is said rather than what is being said.

Allow me to level up with you. I was one of those feeling-base individuals many years ago until I came across an awesome executive coach. His first order of business was telling me that I needed to get my head out of my you know what. Once we got past that, he stated we could begin growing me as a leader. He also said that if I was going to help someone in my company strengthen their leadership ability, and I would at some point, I must help them see themselves as a developing productive brand.

You see, most people are focused on pointing out everyone else's faults or what their company is not doing right. And that's an unproductive waste of free fuel. Unfortunately, not everyone is ready to change or see how great they can become by accepting unvarnished feedback. Trust me; this feedback will not come from a friend, colleague, parent, or boss. They will likely spare your feelings and tell you what you want to hear. If it comes from your boss, they will give you feedback in a corporate, political way, trying to avoid crossing the corporate core values or leadership behaviors.

The victim game has become fashionable. Sadly enough, people only focus on these three things: what's happening, what's happening next, and how they are being treated.

My coach wanted to make sure that I was not focusing on wanting things to get easier but more on making me better. Looking back on my training, it's abundantly clear why he insisted I get into flight school. At the time, I told myself this had nothing to do with me growing as a leader or improving my leadership skills. Now, I can see it clearly. He wanted me to get the excuses out of not being better. You see, when your life depends on your skills being great, you become great fast. My listening and learning abilities became great almost overnight after I entered flight school.

As you can imagine, with flight school, your room for error is narrowed down to a small fraction. Every step in learning is executed to near perfection. Pointing fingers at someone or your company does not fly. You must rely on your knowledge and execution. I became a better leader from the results of learning how to fly. Flying an airplane is a no-excuse mindset.

I often hear people in the workplace complaining or making excuses about everything and not taking accountability or responsibility for what they can do to make things better. Being mad about something trivial while flying can send you to an early grave. Yes, your counterfeit feelings can kill you.

I recommend you build your leadership brand and be an authentic leader. If you have not started, it's a great time to begin reading books. I recommend you read one book a month. I believe in the value of taking my mind to the gym. Another great tool for grounding yourself is skydiving. I can assure you once you make it to the ground, all the things that used to get on your nerves will no longer concern you. You begin to view life and work differently. You will also appreciate what you have rather than what you don't. You will learn to appreciate people at and away from work. It has a way of putting life in perspective.

Self-discovery is often overlooked and misunderstood. When my propeller stopped while flying, I simultaneously discovered fear, courage, a strong mindset, and critical focus. Being the queen or king of sorrow is not a skill set that will bring you home safely if something goes wrong while in the air.

Emotional intelligence is a must-have skill set if you decide to take up flying. In fact, I try to distance myself from people on the ground who don't possess emotional intelligence. They often shoot from the hip when making critical decisions. It is vital that we suspend judgment and gather the facts.

Flying will also teach you to become a sequence thinker. Having an excellent recall memory is a plus. The speed of the right thought can be life or death for you and everyone traveling with you. You may never take up flying. But try to place your actions in the mind of a pilot. You will see an immediate change in how you respond and think.

The stakes are high as we manage through this pandemic. You are required to dig deep and reflect on your training and development. Avoid taking the easy route. Let's face it: anyone with a title and firing power can bully people into doing what they want. However, a skillful leader knows it's about your influence on others. Reaching people wherever they are allows you to lead with a legacy mindset. They will never forget how you made them feel.

Leading others is getting more challenging, as disruption is increasing daily, but you can't develop doubt while managing in a crisis. Be intentional in your pursuit of growing as a leader.

You won't find someone deciding to fly an airplane, get in the air, and say they don't think they can do it. They are fully committed at that point.

Furthermore, if you seek personal growth, you must increase your appetite for discomfort. Start embracing the things you most fear. Your associates are counting on you in many ways. As a reminder, you wear many hats in today's work environment: leader, brother, uncle, father, friend, and mentor if you are in a supervisory role. The company brand is counting on you to be a courageous leader.

# Chapter Thirteen

# The Second Pandemic-Emptiness

The pandemic introduced many people to a new way of coping with uncertainty. Many have been told the environment they are operating in is a part of their new normalcy. They have also been led to believe we are on the other side of this plight. But are we?

Unbeknownst to millions, there's more than uncertainty to deal with. From high IQ to low IQ, it doesn't matter what side of the brain pendulum you operate from; you are feeling some form of trauma. And we all deal with trauma in our own way. As leaders, you must remember that not all wounds are visible. Connecting with people on a meaningful level is not only necessary but critical.

Regardless of what field of work someone is in, they are trying to gain some form of a grounded foundation, be it a stable relationship, work relations, or present or future state. They remain in constant pursuit of stability but keep coming up short. But that's not the most alarming point. It's when they look within for stability and see even less. So, the question becomes, how can an individual deal with this instability without having a personal coach? It is very simple: you must begin in reverse. This concept may come off as being too simple to be true, but it works. Try it for thirty days, and your personal state of being will most likely improve.

Let's begin by not watching television for thirty days. The news can place you in a negative mindset without knowing you have entered that state. Turn off the radio or music in your home or car. If you are going to listen to something at home, in your car, or your earbuds, be selective about what you choose to listen to. I often listen to podcasts of my choosing or light classical music.

Be the first to compliment someone else. This action has a way of placing us in a positive state of mind. It may not make sense to you, but brain chemicals activate, causing you to be positive. Have you ever noticed that people who don't give out compliments always appear to be in a negative mood?

Be content with what you already have. You have never witnessed birds go on strike and decide to stop flying and commit to walking to have Mother Nature produce more worms. They understand the fundamentals of cause and effect. They must get up early or travel a little further if they want more worms. I have learned to eat what's on my plate, which has always served me well.

Learn to calibrate the things around you. Remember, nothing will remain the same. The better you can come to grips with this reality, allows you to become a better version of yourself.

The problem is most people are looking for things in their current environment to remain the same, and that's a troubling metaphor. I have seen this over the years in my line of work. Associates would approach me and say they want to make a lot of money. My reply is that's awesome!! However, they are disappointed when they have to consider a move up within the company or take on greater responsibility.

You don't want to let them down. However, you know something is fundamentally wrong with their chronological path of thinking. As a leader, I'm left with two options: coach them in the moment of how an increase in pay works or take them on as a student and be their personal coach.

Before you laugh at their mindset regarding a pay increase, I was this person many years back. Someone decided to coach me in the moment and became my coach.

Think back to your childhood days when you were able to find simple pleasures. I remember kicking a ball down the road would give me pleasure or climbing a tree. One of my favorite games was sitting by a busy road with a friend, and when a nice car would pass by, we would say, "That's my car." Things have changed today. We are mesmerized by having that new large home, the latest SUV vehicle, or an upgraded iPhone.

If you can transition into finding simple pleasures, you will be happier and mentally more stable. You must do whatever it takes to avoid feeling emptiness. It's a disease that can destroy you. It even causes you to lose your will to perform your best in work and life.

I believe that everyone is capable of achieving the impossible. Gaining control is a process that takes time and practice. Just as getting in shape requires you to work out, changing your state of mind to being more rational and present requires regular stimulation of the right thinking process.

Not everyone is capable of having crucial conversations with themself. That's where an executive coach comes into play.

Can a book serve as an executive coach? Yes. Only if you apply what you have learned. The problem is most people just read without engaging in the process or disagree with trying. What is even more important than knowing what to do is whether or not you will act upon it. The distance between knowing and doing can be substantial, and it can take time for people to get there.

Can the process of getting there go faster? Yes. An executive coach can help you make a quantum leap regarding your progress. The struggle for my executive coach was trying to detach me from my subconscious belief. Contrary to popular belief, you are not the sole contributor to your core values. I learned that the values I was attached to started at a young age. I also learned that my present state of mind was not driving my actions; my core values were.

I share this with you to let you know the journey can be challenging when you are genuinely unaware of who you are—not by name—but by your core values. That is the essence of this chapter: making sense of who you are.

I know that if you fail to understand yourself on a core level, you will continue to operate in a dysfunctional state. Your beliefs are more powerful than your current state of thinking. Now, that's nutritional facts. So. what's my point? I'm trying to remove the carbohydrates from your thinking; the serving size for flawed thinking is plentiful. And you were only worried about the bad calories you placed into your body. You should be more concerned with the bad-thinking calories because they are more permanent and can deleteriously affect your career. When I say no sugar added, I mean it; it's time to distance yourself from bad music, TV viewing, events, and people who can place bad-thinking calories into your mind.

Look, I spent many years being overweight with bad thinking, but I could not see it for myself. I told myself that everyone around me was fat with wrong thinking. I'm sure this did not happen to me overnight.

Have you heard of the term (deception of the gradual) it means something moving at a speed undetected to the human eye. You don't even know that it's taking place. Basically, you transform unbeknownst to yourself.

Fast forward; I'm much more aware of what's entering my mind. You can also develop this skill with a bit of training and consciousness.

# Chapter Fourteen

# Self-Interrogation

Potentiology is by far your greatest asset. It's a made-up word. Here's my definition of the word: the study of self. Nothing could stop you from living a harmonious life if you only knew where the true power lies. Understanding self trumps everything else. The question becomes, what do you know about yourself? This question is the critical starting point for achieving a purpose-filled life.

Self-discovery is often overlooked and misunderstood. Only you know your true strengths and weaknesses, not what someone else has said about what you should become in your career life based on a test you have taken or outwardly limited knowledge. You pose inward intimate knowledge of thyself. This is not to say that an annual review does not have value; many can challenge you to achieve more than what you thought possible if done correctly.

Visualize the things you want to come to fruition. Merriam-Webster defines fruition as the realization of a goal or the end of a plan when success occurs. When you have been planning for something to happen, and it does, this is an example of your plan coming to fruition. Fruition occurs when you burn precisely what you want into your mind. Mental imagery or visualization is a powerful tool. What you focus on will become reality. The clearer you can see something in your mind, the clearer your written goals will be, and the more achievable your goals become.

A few years back, I decided to challenge what I had discovered. I have read many books on goal setting and life skills and observed the behaviors of successful individuals. The principles acquired through my research gave me a quantum leap in my knowledge of building a successful life. My formal education gave me great building blocks for structured success on the job but lacked the life lessons required for independent growth and success. Once I acquired this knowledge, I decided to put it into action; enough with sitting on the bench. I wanted to get into the field of self-discovery and belief in self. With that said, if you are reading this book, I have written two books and invented and patented a product.

I must warn you that how you see yourself is more important than the opinions of your peer group. Good friends and positive-thinking associates are okay. But if you fall into the habit of seeking approval from unworthy peers, it will always be difficult to elevate yourself past their expectations and rise above deceitful value systems.

Strangely, we often strive to seek approval from the people who could care less about us rather than the people who love us for who we are. It is dangerous to give into the notion that the attitudes and opinions of others are more important than your own. A desire to emulate may be considered the norm in given age groups, but do not allow this sway of self-worth to affect your future. Your dreams and your goals are more important than other people's opinions.

For the next few minutes, allow me to be your executive advisor. If you have been blessed with an idea, be it starting a business, bringing a product to market, writing a book, or taking whatever you are doing to the next level, I urge you to act now. The harsh reality is that the world does not reward the average, nor does it reward mediocrity.

Robert Collier said that if you don't make things happen, things will happen to you. Although life isn't always easy, and there are plenty of excuses not to be our best, the rewards go to those who let their actions rise above their excuses. Everyone has good intentions to accomplish many goals, but there lies the problem. You see, we judge ourselves by our intentions, but others judge us by our actions. So, how do you transform from standing still and doing nothing to making a quantum leap toward completing your goal?

You must suspend your judgment of disbelief. Start trusting that the answers will be revered if you genuinely believe in your idea. For example, when I had an idea to write my first book, I did not know where to start. In fact, I didn't even have a title for my book. However, I trusted that the answers would be revered if I had enough courage to act. I began to work in reverse; I searched online for a book publishing company. I even contacted several of them by interviewing them on the phone. Many of the book publishing companies asked me what the title of my book was. I was afraid to tell them that I did not have a title for my book, so I made one up on the spot. In addition, I knew that I would need a professional editing company.

It's been a while since I had to turn in professional grammar work. I repeated the same process to land a professional editing company. I believed in my idea so strongly that I paid a partial payment toward the sum of the total editing fee. I also paid a down payment for the editing work without a title to my book or a completed manuscript.

I started writing different titles for my book on a legal pad. Once I revered the title, I started writing my book. I began designing what I wanted on the front cover of my book. I went on and had some professional photos taken of me as I wanted my picture on the front cover of my book. Yes, I completed the book, and it was a success.

Allow me to digress for a moment. Did you know that bumblebees should not be able to fly? Based on its size, weight, and the shape of its body in relation to the total wingspan, a flying bumblebee is scientifically impossible. The bumblebee, ignorant of scientific input, goes ahead and flies anyway and makes honey every day.

Ignore the sting of negative inputs and thoughts and replace them with positive actions. If you do, you can achieve things no one thinks are possible.

Allow me to be very direct and a little morbid. The last time I visited a graveyard, there were long and short caskets. In other words, both adults and kids were buried there. Don't be the one to talk yourself out of your idea. You don't have as much time as you think.

Those who fear venturing into their ideas don't have many stories to tell. I would rather have ventured out and failed with a story to tell than not have tried.

Here's what I discovered about fear: fear is a physiological and psychological state of mind that narrows vision and limits creativity. Fear can also make you stupid. It compartmentalizes every IQ point into closed loops of worst-case sceneries. Be mindful of your thoughts and make-believe fears. The moral of this tale is that it's about delivering extreme value so that you can enjoy the rest of your time on Earth.

# Chapter Fifteen

# Could Humpty Dumpty Prevent The Fall?

Jim Rohn made a compelling statement when he said, "Work harder on yourself than you do on the job." With that, how much quality time are you devoting to your mental wellness?

A child's cognitive development progresses in distinct stages. At each stage, there are certain abilities and skills that a child needs to master before he or she can progress to the next stage. The learning process moves in steps, each building on the one before. I believe that the sequence of learning for adults is very similar.

Reflecting on my executive training with Dr. Montgomery, I questioned why he could not just tell me what I needed to do to advance myself. His reply was I wouldn't reach my goal without growth. Dr. Montgomery was conscientious about not giving me the answers to the questions I had asked. He preferred that I discover the answers on my own. I realized that Dr. Montgomery's theory on training was he believed that learning is an exploratory process and not something that should be taught. His training style forced me to do more reading and research. In addition, it gave me a quantum leap in my cognitive development skills.

Dr. Montgomery also believes the role of a coach or teacher is not to instruct but to provide the trainee with an environment appropriate to their stage of development. Doing so allows you to discover things as a scientist does by experimentation.

I made the mistake of telling Dr. Montgomery that great things would happen for me if I kept performing well. However, he told me I had to stop being a bystander to my goals and growth. You see, I was seeking changes from the outside world rather than making internal changes. My belief system shaped my perspective.

George A. Kelly stated that we perceive our personality from the inside, from a subjective view, shaping how we see the world. In his personal construct theory, he also said that personality is not inherited or even environmentally shaped but results from cognitive processes. We experience and explore the world, and each of us personally interprets what we discover.

Our interpretations color our subsequent perception and behavior so that we see the world through our own personally constructed "goggles." You consider your frame of reference when choosing what's real to you. This process is also called force carriers. Your interpretation is merely an interpretation of what is essentially an abstract pattern. In addition, 95 percent of the population would rather die than think. People are around you daily, unconscious of their actions, operating on autopilot.

I am often amazed when I see how shocked individuals are from witnessing the results of a person's poor decisions on the news. However, there is a solution to this mindless behavior. As a society, we must focus our efforts on the early ages of individuals.

Social psychology often looks at the basic human need to fit in and calls this the "normative social influence." When we grow up, our moral and ethical compass is almost entirely forged by our environment, so our actions are often a result of the validation we get from society.

If that is true and you're already an adult, you may be thinking, what can you do now to improve your decision-making. Allow me to give you a condensed version of understanding the chronological path to action. This chronological path to action is the inside of your mind in action. If we could open our brains while thinking, this is the process it goes through.

You see, hear, and tell yourself a story; you feel and then act. However, there's a dangerous point in this path to making a decision. It's the story you tell yourself. You begin labeling what you have seen and heard when you tell yourself a story. This labeling establishes love, hate, fear, anger, empathy, and courage. In addition, we generate emotions during this storytelling process.

If you think, no worries, I'm smart; I can make a great choice after telling myself a story. Think again because emotions are more potent than IQ. Once your brain tells itself a story, the next quadrant of thinking goes into autopilot. You are no longer in control of your actions. In essence, the story you tell yourself controls your life.

I highly encourage you to spend the appropriate time developing your mind. Let's face it: what good is it to be alive while being braindead? However, when we are self-aware, we can alter misplaced emotions because we control the thoughts that cause them.

My aha moment came when I discovered the value of self-observation. Self-observation profoundly changes the way our brain works. Self-observation also gives us an incredible amount of control over our feelings. Most of our thoughts and actions are impulsive when we are not self-aware. You see this play out daily in person or on news channels. Yes, the walking dead statement is real.

My intent is to place you in a conscious present state of being. Joy lies there, peace lies there, freedom lies there, and humanity resides here.

Allow me to share a secret with you; nothing is external. However, we tend to have a narrow interpretation of what self-serving behavior entails. You have often heard someone use the term, being in the moment, but are they?

I tend to witness a deluded disconnection of the present state of being. The words come out—I'm here—but the actions demonstrate otherwise. They are about seven mental miles away from where they think they are.

You can create a new you if you can digest what this chapter shares. If you tell me you hope to change, I say do it now because your hopes are most likely nearing retirement. You don't have as much time as you think.

Exposure to things or events allows you to label what you have seen or heard of your own free will. This is where we make meaning of things or, should I say, our interpretation of reality. Hopefully, you are following the path I am taking you on; life and your decisions are a sequence of complex mental algorithms. Get it wrong, and it can lead you down a dark path in life. However, you will live a brighter life if you get it right. My hope is I have provided you with the tools that can place you on the right path to living your best life.

# Chapter Sixteen

# The Experience Self Violates Tradition

The title of this chapter is called the experienced self. With that said, how can you get a grip on the self? One way to better understand the self is to investigate the self from the inside out versus the outside in. Often, our measure of gaining a quantitative understanding of ourselves is done by a visual collection of things. For example, look at the car I drive or my job title; I must be a worthy person. I must be more intelligent than most people. Even better, looking at my degree, others are lazy and worthless. If you use that as your guidepost for understanding yourself, then you are an unconscious individual incapable of knowing your true self.

Now that I have removed your measuring stick to understand the self, the question becomes, what is the self? The self is the person or subject that experiences consciousness. It is me as the subject or self. We cannot observe the self from the outside in the third-person perspective. We can only experience the self from the inside, in the first-person perspective.

Certain thinking styles divide top people from average people. One of them is the difference between informed thinking and uninformed thinking. The other is a controlling factor in our lives, so be mindful of what you say to yourself.

You must also unlearn wrong beliefs. When I was a kid, we were told or heard other people saying, "Sticks and stones will break my bones, but words will never hurt me." However, we found out later that words will kill you. If you hear words, remember they are going somewhere; you must guard your mind. If you hear something often enough, it will eventually take root in you. Death and life are in the power of the tongue.

I have witnessed people give up on their goals and dreams because someone told them it was impossible or no one had done it before. That's death to your goals and or career.

One of the things that you can do to increase the probability of understanding yourself is to cast a wide net. Keep upgrading your knowledge and skills, gathering more information as if your life depended on it because it does. Learn and practice something new each day. Increase the probability of success by increasing the number of dots you connect to create new pictures and generate new ideas, enabling you to achieve more significant goals. New ideas and insights can motivate you to start and keep going until you succeed.

I would be remiss if I did not share this bit of knowledge with you: persistence and determination have always been the most essential qualities for success. As hard as it is, almost anyone can get started, but persevering through thick and thin, continually picking yourself up, and facing failure and disappointment requires your best. When everything in you wants to give up, you must develop the character that will carry you over every obstacle. Vince Lombardi said, "Quitters never win, and winners never quit."

A direct relationship exists between persistence and self-esteem, self-respect, and personal pride. The more you discipline yourself to persist in the face of adversity, the more you will like and respect yourself, and the more powerful you will feel. Your subconscious mind or self is *potent*. In fact, you can pre-program it, like setting an alarm clock to go off for you how you want it to. If you want to become successful, you can program your mind in advance to *never* give up. The way you do this is simple: you say to yourself, "No matter what happens, I will *never* give in."

After reading this chapter, you will *never* be the same person. You have encountered a mental graduation toward correct thinking and action. If you revert to being the old you after learning to be a better self, it's on you.

When I was a little kid, my mother used to tell me, "It's okay to do wrong if you don't know what is right, but it's not okay to do wrong if you know what's right."

My hope is that you are reading this chapter without bias and trying to understand what I am trying to convey to you. However, I can clearly understand if you disagree or reject my theory on personal programming. In addition, I know it's tough to see things from another person's perspective without proof of results. Yes, becoming a better version of yourself takes time and practice. However, if you engage in this reprogramming of the mind and structured thinking, you will make discoveries and improvements. What you must avoid is being locked into your biases, as they can have a detrimental effect on your well-being and goals. This crucial conversation may be a game changer in your life and career. I know because I have tested this method in my life.

I stated this before. However, it's worth mentioning again. My executive coach Dr. Robert Montgomery introduced me to this way of thinking, which profoundly impacted my life. The best way I can describe it to you is when I adopted this way of thinking, it felt like someone else had stepped into my body. I was a completely different person.

If you don't feel this chapter or book adds value, stop reading it now and place it on a shelf. However, please hold on to it and pass it to someone you feel can use it. We are all at different stages in our lives and careers, and at some point, you may decide it's time to focus on improving yourself from the inside out.

I have a question: what do you feel when I ask if you are complete? By now, your feelings have started to come into play, and you are searching for wholeness without substance. If you cannot transform yourself, that means you are a few steps away from a mental breakdown. You are under an illusion trying to separate I from me. No one wants to be the wrong I, but rather a better me.

You see, when you speak, it's silence; when it speaks, you are silent. You can't control your thoughts or feelings; they happen without input. However, your reaction after they take place is critical. Anxiety, anxiousness, rush to judgment, and panic are byproducts of not being able to slow down the speed of your misplaced emotions. Try implementing these newfound skills; I assure you this will change who you are.

Most people just react; this is an auto-response behavior that you can learn to control or, should I say master. I am here to defy a myth; you can change at any age. Stop allowing others to tell you that you can't change at this age or why change now. You have been doing it this way for years. Most people who make those statements have not had an original thought in years.

Beware of people with preformulated thoughts, as they have been known to kill dreams, ideas, goals, and your ability to excel. They remind me of the words I hear in TV advertisements: *we conducted a double-blind test*. Why do they need to try and convince the masses of their product by making that statement? It reminds me of a comment that one of my sisters used to make when someone called her out on something. She used to say, "I bet you I did not do that or take that, I bet you." At that point, we all knew she did it. For the simple fact, she was trying too hard to convince us that she was in the right. As a family, we often look back and laugh about her behavior at that time. However, there was a valuable lesson in that juvenile behavior. Look for the vabel mass that someone is about to place over your eyes when they are adamant about their claim.

# Chapter Seventeen

# I Don't Like Leaf Shine

Making a plant look great by adding leaf shine does serve its purpose. You can take a dull-looking plant and make it look amazing with the right amount of Leaf Shine added to the leaves of a plant. For clarity, Leaf Shine is a brand name. I am not speaking ill of the product or its ability to perform; I'm simply making a leadership point about how the process of Leaf Shine weakens a leader's ability to perform at their best. The product happens to tie in nicely to proving my point. With that said, you can dress up as a leader and speak the right words, and in the right environment, you can perform well and look amazing for a period, but what happens when a plant's soil is not watered or properly fertilized? Well, that's what's happening today in many workplaces.

Leaders sound and look good without the foundation for pouring into their people. Things have changed for the associates in many ways. To be more direct, they need your compassion, understanding, encouragement, and inspiration. Today's climate is very different from two years ago. The associates are running on reserve if you have not figured it out. In fact, none of us are at our full potential. The soil is dry, and fertilizer is lacking, yet we put on our best shine (smile) every day.

Let's stay on this journey of plant life just in case you wonder why or how a tree planted outside survives on its own. There are two reasons for that thought. A mature tree has most likely weathered many storms, including droughts and floods, and depending on the region, withstood hurricanes and is still standing. Second, it's supported by other strong trees nearby; yes, trees support one another.

I was born and raised in Florida; I have witnessed palm trees appear at a 45-degree angle during a hurricane, only to find that same palm tree standing back upright after the storm. In addition, I have witnessed small trees in a hurricane that appeared not to have been affected at all by the storm. In these two scenarios, the mature trees took on the brunt of the storm for the smaller trees. The mature trees knew the smaller trees did not have an established root system to withstand the storm. There's a biblical term to support my rationale: standing in the gap.

Now, let's put this into people's terms. If you have been blessed to have had an executive coach at some point in your career, you are an established person who can take on the high winds of the work environment. With that said, your mission should be to take on a supportive role and help coach and guide the less-tenured or established associates during turbulent times. Their roots are not deep and can easily be uprooted.

If the trees understand this simple and yet supportive role, my question to you is, what's wrong with you? We allow far too many associates to fall victim to disciplinary actions up to termination. Looking back on my career path, I had a lot of supportive trees around me. I can assure you without those mature trees, I would have failed.

Those trees supported me when my roots had just been established. I am amazed to see people pull up a plant out of the pot and trash it just because they spotted a few brown leaves when, in fact, all it needed was a little nourishment to get that plant back to its full potential.

I was full of brown leaves during my first two or three years in retail. I encourage you to set your sights on improving the welfare of others; believe me, it will pay dividends. I am living proof of many people pouring into me. If you are in a leadership position, I challenge you to become a change-maker and make a difference. The decisions you make today will negatively or positively impact others for many years to come. Yes, your roots run deep.

Impactful leadership teaches people how to think, and they will find the leader within themselves. But if you tell them what to do, they will remain followers throughout their careers. Once you get them in thinking mode, they will discover that the mind and the brain are different.

When you change your mind, your brain will change as well. Remember, it's the mind that changes the brain. You activate your brain by instructing the mind.

I must confess I have worked with a few leaders who clearly had their brains switched off. Yes, your brain can still function without the use of your mind. Most of what we do daily does not require thinking but rather doing. I'm sure you have heard the term "absent-minded," meaning people are lost in thought and unaware of their surroundings or actions. Being preoccupied with a fear of someone thinking is a slow death to the individual and your company.

Allow me to give you an example of not using your mind. Have you ever driven to your local store, picked up a few items, and returned home only to realize that what you went for did not come back with you? You were on brainpower. If you were on mind power, you would have been thinking and come back with the item you went to purchase.

It's time for you to revise what you think. Let your brain know that you are back in the present mode of thinking. There's a happy feeling associated with understanding the power of your mind. You will also feel elated knowing what you can achieve. When I say achieve, I'm not speaking of remembering the items you were supposed to pick up at the store. This outcome of mind control is on a quantum frequency level. It's hard for me to describe what you will experience, but I can share that it is beneficial in many ways. Accept the venture of knowing for yourself. Once you have arrived, you will often question why moving in this direction took so long.

There's truth and logic that goes with the phrase "facts over feelings." However, far too many individuals live their lives in a feeling and emotional-based logic lifestyle. Yes, I called it a lifestyle because that's where they have chosen to spend their mental time.

If you disagree with anything I have presented in this chapter, at least agree with the reality that you don't have as much time on this planet as you think you have. You must stop wasting precious years of your life in mental suspense mode. Allow yourself to think differently because freedom is around the corner.

My closing question for this chapter is, have you ever slowed down enough to realize how many things are competing for your energy? I say free yourself.

Unbeknownst to many people, they function at 80 percent brain power. Can you imagine the possibilities if you operated 80 percent mind power and 20 percent brain power? Your results will surprise you. I'm living proof of this 80/20 rule.

I used to collect empty aluminum cans off the street and sell them to an aluminum company for money. Why? Because I did not know how to operate my mind. My brain was functioning, but my mind was absent.

Allow me to clarify something before you connect the wrong mental dots. Establishing wealth does not determine whether you are operating on mind power. I have conversed with many wealthy people in my life only to realize they were functioning on brain power. Being wealthy does not require using your mind. You could be wealthy via winning the lottery, family inheritance, purchasing company stock at an opportune time, or simply being in the right place at the right time. On the other hand, I have conversed with janitors, maids, and retail workers only to discover that they were speaking from the standpoint of full mind power. Believe me, you know it when you hear it.

One sign to determine if they have "full mind power" is speaking from a place of peace. That's worth more than any monetary value you can earn. There are more significant attributes of operating on full mind power. However, I thought this was a great place to start without getting into a deeper discussion of the power of your mind.

You would be accurate if you said I was on a mission to free people from their brains. There are some benefits to operating on brain power. However, I don't believe that 80 percent of brain power is useful. Reduce it to 20 percent and watch how you transform from the outside in. Yes, I said it correctly—from the outside in.

You must come to terms with this equation. You can't believe something is possible until you start acting that way. Show yourself that you are doing what you believe, and your mind will follow. Let's face it: you have placed a lot of stuff into your mouth over the years, not knowing its actual ingredient or effect on your body. With that said, why can't you put the information I've given you into your mind and try it? The worst that can happen is you go back to being yourself.

Let's be clear: this is not a "fake it until you make it" concept but rather doing it until your mind believes that you are onboard or all-in. The mind knows your brain will convince you that it's not possible. But you can override that inner conversation by engaging in the action as if you are an expert in what you desire to achieve. The rest of the details will come together like completing a 1000-piece puzzle. The subtle impact of this action is your confidence will explode. You will accomplish every goal you set forth to achieve once you engage in the action with full mind acceptance. Period!

# Chapter Eighteen

# Avoid Uneven Pavements

Birth to childhood is fascinating. We are eager to learn at a rapid pace. In addition, our curiosity is at its peak. With a fresh mindset, nothing could stop us from learning, growing, understanding processes, and figuring things out. With that, somewhere along the way, we lose our zeal for knowledge and winning. Unbeknownst to many of us, our minds go on an unhealthy learning diet.

Of course, this is not the case for everyone. A percentage of people are entrenched in continuous learning. However, if your quest for mental growth has run low or evaporated, I recommend you do whatever it takes to regain that burning desire for understanding. The longer you wait, the more you are unlikely to do anything about it. Your passion for learning will appear to be a galaxy away from engaging.

If you are unaware of where to start on this journey of reengaging your mind, I first recommend reading a book a month. With access to audible books, this is possible. Second, search for a mentor, coach, or executive coach. Depending on your level of leadership, each one of these coaches matters. Running alongside someone is better than being dragged alongside someone. That's what it feels like when you fall behind in an industry or branch of knowledge. And last, ask a friend, family member, or coworker to be your accountability partner. Set some goals for yourself and share them with this chosen individual. Here's my disclaimer: ensure this person is in your corner. If not, their feedback could place you in a reverse mindset.

Our childhood fears are often our adult behaviors. The wrong advice can trigger your mind to work against you. I've been there, feeling like I was mentally drowning. Friends and family members don't always make the best mentor. They will often spare your feelings, which will hinder you from true growth.

My executive coach delivered me the unvarnished truth without sparing my feelings. That's not to say that he was always putting me down. His inspiration was always inserted at the right time and place as if he was a surgeon conducting a mental operation. I needed to take you on this journey to explain my true intentions.

Most companies are transitioning at a fast pace and for the right reasons. Let's face it: competition never sleeps. If a company is not growing, then it is decaying. Too many companies have fallen victim to trying to dog-paddle their way to the other side, which is growth. It's the fast that eats the slow.

You, as an individual must get the "F" word out of your mouth. There is no finish line in business; you must have a growth mindset. With that, how are you growing mentally? If the company you work for is developing and growing fast but you are not, that's uneven pavement—the surface cracks when one side rises and the other does not. Your walk with that company will not go smoothly. Get out of your feelings and get into action. No one wants to hear about what you will do but will observe your actions.

People often tell me what they will do or how passionate they are about their work, projects, or goals with no evidence of their words. Yes, I just turned into your executive coach for a brief moment. I am not concerned with what happened to you as a child or your plight in life. I am concerned with keeping you employed as well as accomplishing your goals. I am also willing to walk alongside you as long as you demonstrate the desire to win.

Most people have forgotten how to believe. With that loss of belief, they have not had an original thought in years. They are living life as a copy rather than an original. Try being an original and watch your life soar.

Do not take fun out of your learning. If you do, the pain will seep into your feelings, dictating your emotions and making you feel bad about learning. Learning should always have an element of fun built into it. You will experience a quantum leap in your retention level if it does. If you need some personal words of inspiration, tell yourself that you look forward to life's challenges and have mentally prepared for the journey. I genuinely believe your joy comes from the labels you place on what you may see or hear. Those labels will bring you joy or pain. Death and rebirth lie within our thoughts.

With that, be watchful of what you are mentally eating. It's not always about the things that go into our mouths that decay us. That's only one facet of it. Faster deterioration comes from what's eating you mentally.

Meeting someone I have inspired to fight a little harder through my words brings me joy.

Be mindful of the narrative you are telling yourself. My mother was an example of a great fighter; she raised seven kids as a single parent while working two or three jobs. I knew many days, she would go to bed hungry so that we could eat. I also learned as a young kid how to fight through tears and fears while moving forward.

I established two jobs in middle school, but these jobs did not bring in much money. However, giving my mother the proceeds from my day's work made me feel closer to manhood. On the weekends, I would collect aluminum cans and scrap metal and sell them to the scrap yard for a nominal fee. I also discovered that bottles were going for ten cents a bottle—another cash flow job. A kid in my neighborhood turned me onto my fourth way of earning money—helping customers load groceries into their cars. However, this grocery store was far from my apartment building.

My mother thought I was riding my bike to a friend's house two streets from where we lived. This gig turned out to be the most lucrative. I decided to turn my younger brother onto it after he declared to go public to our mother if I did not let him in. We became business partners that day, as I was unwilling to give up this lucrative gig.

Allow me to explain better what I meant when I said I had to fight through the tears and fears while moving forward. At the end of our block, two older boys were neighborhood bullies. On my way to earn money, I often fought both simultaneously. Yes, they got the best of me in some of those fights. However, that would not stop me from going after what I wanted. I kept this a secret from my mother, not wanting her to worry about my well-being as she had enough on her plate raising us.

She eventually discovered I was in a fight when I came home wearing one shoe and ripped pants. While fighting those brothers, I lost one of my shoes and could not locate it after the fight. I share this story, not wanting anyone to feel sorry for me.

The weekly sparring with those brothers made me a better athlete as I entered sports in school. Without them allowing me to practice with them, I don't think that I would have become as great of an athlete as I was in football and wrestling. Wrestling became my greatest sport as I was used to dealing with two people simultaneously instead of one. This became a benefit in karate as well. I had already made up my mind that no one could hurt me. Karate was a fun sport for me. On a funny note, I did not have to worry about losing a shoe as this was a barefoot sport.

I was also able to develop physical and mental toughness from my altercation with those brothers. Not all experiences are bad; the label you place on your experience gives it meaning.

# Chapter Nineteen

# Whales Land on A Beach

Business and personal growth can be an exhilarating mental ride. Some of your most significant memories will stem from the ride of growth.

Businesses will share that same experience on their journey to becoming relevant in the marketplace. When a personal goal becomes realized, endorphins are released in the brain. Learning a new skill or discovering your ability to perform at a higher level will leave a positive, lasting impression for years.

Allow me to go in a different direction. Normal behavior will produce average to little results.

Learn to swim in deep waters. Even if you are not a great swimmer, take the chance.

Our ability to scale lies within our thoughts. If you believe you are limited, your results will come from the actions of your thoughts. That is not to say that times won't be tough. Choppy water does occur at unexpected times. Can you travel with a life vest, and if so, what does it look like in business?

A life vest in business is developing mental toughness. Believe me, you will need it somewhere along the way. If you fail to develop this mental toughness, you could experience an emotional breakdown and lose the ability to seek a better outcome for your life. The question becomes: who's going to love you now? The answer has to be yourself.

External things, including monetary accomplishments, won't be enough to satisfy your soul. You will start filling that void with stuff—cars, homes, relationships, and careers. However, you will visit that place at a time you are unprepared for.

I am encouraging you to discover what matters most to you now. Don't go another day without engaging in this mind-provoking quest for fulfillment. If you ignore this advice, you will find yourself on the highway of life with no exit ramp.

It feels awesome to set goals and targets, knowing that you are meeting your expectations. BINGO! You feel like a whale in the ocean, conquering any and everything you have a desire for. It's also comforting knowing that you have no predators around you. Checkmate, right? You are coasting, and the ocean belongs to you.

Before you agree with that statement, I must remind you we can be fooled by predictable patterns, believing that we are invincible, allowing our actions to take us to the edge. Yes, whales do land on the beach. And without the proper human intervention, they will most likely end their life there. As individuals, we often run into similar situations.

If you fail to acquire a reinvention coach, your career life will die prematurely. Coaches, Mentors, executive coaches, and reinvention coaches are worth more than monetary exchange. They will put the much-needed oxygen back into your lungs.

Getting off track is easy when you feel you are on the right course. I recommend you invest in yourself before you are advised to seek help. More importantly, avoid waiting on the calvary. Also, seek advice, not opinions.

You must be strategic when it matters most; you don't have time to waste when landing on the sand. Mistakes do happen to the best of us. No one is insulated from mishaps in life and career. Your ability to get back up is more important than the fall. Believe me, I have failed many times in my career.

A few times when I failed, I tasted the dirt. However, I was able to reinvent myself and get back on track. Pride and ego will fill your mouth with dirt. Let go and be open to change. If you are just beginning your career, most of this dialogue will sound like hocus pocus to you. In other words, it doesn't make any sense. Just keep working; it will become crystal clear at some point. The great news is I have given you the tools and techniques to better prepare yourself for any encounter.

Learn from others' mistakes when they offer you the path of least resistance at no charge. I say take it!

# Chapter Twenty

# It's Coming

We are responsible for leading the younger generation through turbulent times, modeling integrity leadership behaviors, and providing foundational tools for wise decision-making. However, we often feel like everything is going well for them, or we feel unworthy of our great responsibilities as leaders.

The temptation most new leaders struggle to overcome is the need for approval—affirmation or adoration from those around them. They seek respect from their members, recognition from coworkers, and good standing within their community. We all long for acceptance, so we shift our attention to the accolades the workplace so teasingly offers.

Perhaps we didn't get the approval we needed from our families. Or maybe we know we are inwardly more fragile than the lofty expectations we have placed upon ourselves. Being in the spotlight does bring its own set of complexities. With that, our priorities can become misguided.

As a leader, you have a remarkable twofold responsibility. First, you are called to embrace the company policy and procedure wherever you are, making the grace and truth of the company the central component of your role. Second, you are called to share the great qualities of the company you serve with anyone who comes across your path.

We could be lured into believing that compassion for others is not worth it in the workplace, or our coworkers could cause us to grin without caring. I urge you not to take that bait, as the consequences can have adverse effects. Staying alert and on course isn't just for your survival. It impacts the generation that follows you.

You have often heard your subordinates will mimic your leadership style once they are in charge of others. I'm speaking from experience.

I know what it is to be in need and what it is to have plenty. I have learned the secret of being content in any and every situation, whether well-fed or hungry for knowledge. However, I will say our decision-making and leadership are better when we learn to be content, no matter the outcome. Here's my question to you: are you willing to sacrifice?

I promise you will become devoted to your rich and satisfying life sometime along your career journey. Let me remind you of this simple yet powerful act: together, we transform our lives and live with more power and purpose than we ever could alone.

At some point in your career, you may have been blessed to help someone deserving of that same amazing lifestyle you have enjoyed. Let no one, and I mean no one, despise you for doing what's right by an individual. Be an ambassador of change. Tell anyone who will listen about the incredible transformation you went through to become a leader of people. You're encouraged to explain that such transformation is also available to them. You have an endless supply of stories to tell. More importantly, it lets others know their importance to the company.

True progress comes from seizing the invitation to take risks, where the rewards of risk-taking can lead to the satisfying life we were all created to live.

To be transparent, it took me time to develop the skills of a disciplined leader. With that being said, if you are willing to invest in yourself, life has a way of giving back to you in a meaningful way. If you did not connect the dots, the unspoken words are: vision is mission critical.

Everything starts with visualizing yourself living in the future of what you desire to do or be. Yes, there is tremendous value in viewing life through the lens of trajectory. I encourage you to reject the notion that everything is a fixed construct. What's important to understand is that the internal visual choices you make today impact the pathways for tomorrow, and life is not merely what our eyes can see. So, what you should do, once you have arrived, is to ascribe to walking with integrity and character, as it is the hallmark of great leadership.

Your second mission as a leader of people is to work toward modeling what great leadership looks like in action. I try not to be disingenuous in my assessment of leadership.

I live in this world, and I am part of this world. With that, there is a crisis in leadership today. Leaders must become involved in the success of others. The mantra of I got it on my own, so others must get theirs" can't be the mantra of the work environment. Allow your deeds to speak louder than your words. Having a genuine care for the welfare of others is embodied in great leadership. Learning to put others first and treat them with respect takes courage.

This second quality leadership attribute is challenging to execute because we all operate in an ever-increasing, fast-paced environment with high demands for returns. Mature leaders seek to grow by pouring themselves out for the development of their subordinates while continuously driving profitability. These are a few characteristics that describe the mark of a great leader. Become unapologetic about your aspiration to be the best leader you can be.

# Chapter Twenty-One

# Stop Eating from Baby Jars

Understanding the paradox of supremacy leadership is only known by a select few. Many will claim they possess the knowledge but do not truly understand what it takes to demonstrate those deeds. Many are unwilling to submit to mentorship, which leads to knowledge without understanding. You can only lead as far as you were led. The task of leadership is, without a doubt, filled with heart-wrenching, self-defeating moments of burnout. However, it can be one of the most fulfilling journeys of your life.

Training for a marathon is the more appropriate stance when you commit to being a servant leader. There are many blind spots when first becoming a leader, and your ego is at the top of that list. Second, you must mature.

New leaders often have a shallow definition of great leadership. I recommend finding solid leaders to surround yourself with early in your career. Growth occurs by being with leaders who will support and challenge you. The character of a great leader takes time to ripen.

I challenge you to explore your desire and intentions to become a leader. To begin, remove pay from the list and pick another reason for your quest to lead people. Being mindful of your motives will help lead you on the correct path. Center your aim on the people as they will drive the metrics. In an age of "what's in it for me" (WIIFM), we can lose our reason for becoming a leader in translation of running a profitable business.

This next point is worth the purchase of this book. As leaders, we tend to lean toward one of two extremes with ourselves: over-discipline or under-discipline. Some of us naturally tend to be over-disciplined because we strive for perfection. With that being said, we often seek to maintain order at the expense of being harsh with ourselves and those around us. Taking on a posture of anxiety robs you of the beauty of leading in the present.

Working each day with a zeal for growth is the best mindset a leader can seek to achieve. Although I remain a work in progress, I commit to immersing myself in the person I choose to become. That mindset allows me to exemplify the quest governing my leadership. However, it would be disingenuous of me if I did not share the other side of being a leader with you. It can be discouraging and lonely, and there can be a bit of despair at times. The one thing we can fall back on is our moral compass during those moments of leading through difficult seasons.

Another one of the secret lessons I operate by is called the "to-be project." Write down whatever you want to become or happen in your life. Immerse yourself in the possibilities of what is possible. Believe me, it works. I have put this format to the test many times with real results.

At some point, you must decide to stop eating from baby jars. You must transition from operating from the standpoint of what you have been fed to what you have discovered. That's when the infinite possibilities take hold. You will manifest what the heart desires. There's a shift in your energy when you live in what can be instead of what has already happened.

Everything you need is within you; make no mistake about it. Unbeknownst to many, your outcome is based on what you have witnessed others doing. Yes, you are a habit-producing human being.

Originality is fading fast in our society. I believe indiscriminate elements of engagement tend to be the norm in how we operate.

Allow me to share this unspoken truth about you: your full potential self is looking to escape the mental you holding you back. It takes guts to face what you are capable of achieving.

I have a simple question for you: are you driven or being dragged? You have to come to terms with this question.

Often, I hear individuals speak a great game. However, their actions are far from what they claim to be about. You are doing yourself a disservice when your deeds don't match your words. I only coach those who are willing to be honest with themselves. Otherwise, find or hire a liar who's willing to mentor you.

Your ability to punch above your weight class is a factor of discipline and grit.

I used to think the algorithm for success was based on what Ivy League school you attended or possessing a high IQ. Of course, those two factors can help you along the way, but it's not a guarantee that you will become successful. Being intelligent, lazy, and having a pedigree background will only get you so far. In addition, it works well for you when things are normal.

Have you ever encountered an ambush? I only ask this question because if you haven't, chances are one is coming.

Let me be clear: I am not against Ivy League schools, as I believe they have their place.

If you have lived a little, you will most likely agree with the statement that despair will visit you without your invitation, and it brings along elements of chaos. However, having an executive coach will help you look around those dark corners of what's to come and how to deal with the elements of surprise that life brings. Notice I did not say that having an executive coach will be a panacea for your life.

I shared this in an early chapter. However, it's worth sharing again. When I was in flight school, while flying a single prop airplane with my instructor, the propeller stopped while we were seven thousand feet in the air. Well, you already know the outcome of this story because I wrote this book. The moral of this story is that he got the propeller back in rotation due to his experience with these types of troubled situations. His experience was not a guarantee; we could have both had a fatal outcome. He's my learned leadership takeaway from that experience while in the air. My instructor was focused, disciplined, resilient, and determined to get us to the ground safely and alive. His actions will be forever etched into my memory.

I encourage you to take advantage of the free lessons out there. Establish a relationship with an elementary school teacher. They possess more discipline, grit, and resilience than many leaders you will come across. Another person to befriend is a nurse. They understand hard work and are prepared, disciplined, and consistent in what they do. These are just a few. I challenge you to open up your relationships and conversations with others outside your profession; it can grow you immensely. I make it a habit to conversate with others outside of my profession. You can pick up a ton of valuable nuggets beneficial to business and your leadership.

Never underestimate the power of networking; being in a silo can have an adverse effect on your operations. I also try to keep a close ear to the street because listening to what is said in the local barber shop or salon has merit. The conversations are wide and varied in these locations, ranging from the latest clothes trends to politics.

Now, I must add a disclaimer: you must go into these buildings with a fine filter on what is being said. Knowing how to discern between fact and fiction is critical. However, there is value in what is being circulated.

# Chapter Twenty-Two

# Unconscious in Plain Sight

Understanding your associates' mindset and intentions before they play out regarding work and dedication to the brand is priceless. Every organization or corporation is in pursuit of this knowledge. If I had to place a monetary sum to this knowledge, I would say it's in the millions, if not billions. Why? Actions in the right direction with momentum is a force field that is almost impossible to stop. Knowing how to channel your associates' or team members' efforts and energy is powerful.

Think of it this way: when you direct energy in the same direction, it's called electricity, and it powers cars, homes, buildings, and cities. However, the wrong usage of that same energy can be deadly. I am not aware of anyone who has grabbed a bare 220-volt plug and is able to talk about it. The critical point is we are putting leaders in place without the proper gloves or tools to deal with 220 volts of live or exposed wires.

Remember when I told you your associates are energy and electricity for your organization or brand? There is a shift taking place in the workplace that is unbeknownst to many leaders and executives. What if I told you I had the secret to channeling the energy of your associates? More importantly, what if I told you it's a free formula?

The sad reality is that you will not take this formula seriously because I told you it was free and requires very little engagement or actions by your leaders. However, if I told you it would cost you $500,000 for this acquired knowledge, you would most likely be willing to pay me this sum and believe every word I shared with you on this powerful energy-forced multiplier. The question becomes, can your company afford not to possess this knowledge?

Now, if you think I am seeking some form of monetary value for this knowledge, you are wrong. I am simply proving my case.

Before engaging fully in its actions, I will discuss some components of what it takes to begin this thought process. A leader must be generous with their identity and share with their team members their shortcomings and what they have failed at, as no one is without fault. There is something about being a leader willing to discuss their failure and how they overcame it. You see, generosity seems to work in two ways. We get to give gifts to others while we receive the pleasure of being generous.

No two days are the same if you operate in the retail arena. Predictable outcomes will not be the norm. However, you must be committed to the journey because the people you manage rely on you. A critical component of leadership when things are less predictable is to help your people build the self-image of a winner. This is a vital skill set to acquire for the individuals on your team. Here's why. Let's say someone has a talent of 8 on a scale of 1-10, but their self-image is a 4. When under pressure, we can only perform to our self-image rather than the level of our talent or intellect. This fact remains a secret to many. Our self-image is stronger than our talent.

Self-esteem or self-belief is closely linked to the neurotransmitter serotonin. When we severely lack serotonin, it can lead to depression, self-destructive behavior, or even suicide. In addition, social validation is real.

Great leaders understand that people deal with pain and problems differently. There are five other critical components to understanding individuals' human consciousness and mindset. However, I am not going to discuss it in this chapter, knowing that many will not view the total algorithm of understanding the behaviors of our actions as revealed in plain sight. Yet, I will let you in on one of the five remaining ingredients. Leaders must retrain their ears. Leaders with trained ears hear more than the average leader. Remember, nothing is hidden anymore; we just need to retain our eyes and ears to witness what's already in plain sight.

Here's a sneak peek into what you may or may not know: everyone shops for satisfaction. However, acquiring new things is not the solution. Many will subscribe to a pattern of thinking that if they just buy X, they'll have all they need. The truth of the matter is boxed up in believing that our fulfillment comes from what we have when, in fact, everything we need resides within all of us. It does not come from an external object. I hope you discover sooner rather than later in life that our strength is found in the simplicity of our needs.

One of the most complex challenges you will face in life is unlocking your mind. For example, if you are looking for a fantasy, you believe a nightmare exists. We often try to distance ourselves from what we think will bring us pain. This nightmare is a mental illusion stored somewhere in our brains. However, we feel it will find us if we don't locate the opposite. With that, we begin the mental and physical journey of chasing happiness because we feel sadness will get us. We chase love because we think hate will visit us. We seek pleasure because we fear pain will enter our lives.

Imagine if you could stop this seeking and avoidance mindset; how much more stable would you be as a human being? I lost valuable and unproductive years not understanding this simple brain game. However, once I acquired this knowledge, social validation became nonexistent. I am not moved by external views or opinions of others unless it has honest intent with meaningful value. My goal is to equip you with this same skill set. You have the tools required. It's up to you to download and believe in what you are capable of. That's a mental fact you can live with for life.

I leave you with this thought: is time moving, or are we mentally moving? I'll give you my thoughts on this question in another chapter. I believe that speed is internal rather than external.

You may wonder what quantum theory has to do with you as an individual or leader. If you are not connecting the dots, you are most likely experiencing pain or pressure on your job. As humans, we have the innate ability to resolve complex matters with ease.

Also, anxiety is locked within the mind by you rather than by an external situation or event. However, the great news is you can edit pain in real-time. Think about it; you must tell yourself that you are upset or should be upset by a situation. I don't waste time placing myself in places I choose not to be, and you should practice that same mindset. For what it's worth, life does not last as long as you want it to or believe it will. I urge you to choose a happier path. If your head is underwater, you are not breathing well.

# Chapter Twenty-Three

# Perception of Reality

Don't become a victim of always learning but never being able to come to the knowledge of the truth. Don't just learn the facts; try to gain insight from the knowledge acquired. To scale and separate from the average, you must ascertain value-added secrets while dismantling workplace myths. Your thoughts guide the trajectory of your career.

Many people struggle to adjust to changes on the job. The path of perseverance begins with understanding the facts, not feelings. I am amazed by the amount of energy individuals place on things they can't change, such as someone else's attitude or a new policy on the job. Misguided energy will keep you confused for many years with no progress in your growth.

There is zero value in coaching yourself. Allow me to be honest with you. I tried coaching myself for many years. I had significant momentum going at high speed. But the problem was I was on a hamster wheel, moving without achievement. The narrative I told myself was that as long as I had motion, I must be doing something right. That was the biggest fallacy I could have told myself. With that said, don't mistake movement for achievement.

Reading this book is an excellent sign of the urgency toward improving your perception. I hope you find the strength and perseverance to continue growing and not fall back on your understanding of the matters at hand. Your world will change almost immediately once you get into a winning mindset.

Our perceptions of what is real have always manipulated our actions. There's another side of this coin that we often keep in silence. Our insecurity and pride keep us from being our authentic selves. I was able to overcome my insecurities by being willing to be vulnerable. I'm willing to admit what I don't know and what I don't understand. I will remain a student as long as I'm in the present. Do yourself a favor and stop pretending to have mastered work; there are too many moving parts in a given day at work, not to mention the unintended ambushes that can be present at any given moment.

Allow me to talk about an unspoken topic. Things will never get easier on the job, so let's be clear. You must learn to handle challenges better. Or I can suggest you learn to get better. My executive coach advised me, "You must increase your appetite for discomfort to master any given skill set." I used to wish for things to improve until I learned this, and it was a game changer. Now, I work hard on myself in silence, not wishing for life or things to get easier.

You acquire mental resilience by dismantling old, wishful-thinking belief mechanisms and replacing them with what is possible. You are a mobile think tank of incredible possibilities. However, you cannot ascertain those possibilities through unconscious motion. Yes, motion can take place without thinking. You see accounts of this on your local news channel every day. It's almost as if we have moved to a society of drone thinkers.

Who controls your thinking and actions? Remember, if you don't control your thoughts, you don't control your actions.

It's time to go back home; let the old you be dead and gone.

Now that you understand mindless momentum better, I encourage you to take a different approach to engaging with others. Turn the light in your brain on and enjoy the benefits of a newer version of yourself. Alternatively, stay on the current path you've been on, as I'm sure it's bringing you tremendous joy in your life.

I'm jealous that I didn't find this knowledge sooner. I'm also reminded that there's no refund for regrets in life. Many of us have been on this mental highway without an exit. Cars must exit the highway to refuel or for a check-up. With that said, your mind must receive a mental check-up as well. You can't continue to travel without processing what's going on. Well, you can? Just don't expect to feel satisfaction or pleasure in your long-term choices.

Yes, you can feel good, but good is not the same as feeling great. Many people will convince you to feel good about your actions. However, you know yourself better than anyone else.

I ask you, why live a deodorized life? It's time to start dealing with what is being covered up. I understand it's painful to deal with the inner self, so you keep pretending to be someone other than yourself. If you can't be true to yourself, don't expect to be true to anyone else. If you are in love with who you are, then I don't recommend you change. That's not to say that what you are doing will go without future consequences, just keep playing the hand you're dealing to others without feelings.

Yes, you must manage others if that's your role. However, there's good and bad engagement in everything we do in work and life. So, why is there so much confusion going on in our brains? Is it by our design or the environment we're in?

Here's a better question to ponder: can you gain control of this accelerated mental movie in your mind? Continue to follow me on this journey.

This may come as a surprise, but thinking is not real. We're under an illusion if we think we are thinking. Your choices have been removed from you many years ago. You're involved in a live hypnotic state of mind. The sad state of affairs on this topic is many are unaware of how to go back to thinking on their own for this simple yet true statement. We have conditioned ourselves to believe that lying to ourselves is something good.

I ran across this research that I believe has a lot of merit. It stated that "2 percent of the population think, 3 percent think they think, and 95 percent of the population would rather die than think." Most of the actions we engage in are programmed behaviors.

Think about all of the chaos that is taking place in the world. Do you believe people are thinking? Let's bring this question closer: when did you last have an original thought? Don't tell me you thought about going to the gym today or started a diet last year and lost thirty pounds. Again, those activities don't require any thinking; they were most likely imparted to you some years ago.

I challenge you to name something that you have done that required thinking. This exercise is not to make you feel bad about yourself but rather involve you in reverse thinking to provoke your ability to think again.

I engaged in this process and ended up writing and self-publishing three books. Prior to learning how to unwire and reprogram my brain, I was just going through the motions.

As you started reading this chapter, I already began the mental work on you. You may not understand it. But everything is mental. I have done the initial work on you. Now, it's time for you to take it to the next level; it requires your involvement.

Did you know that desire and expectancy is a powerful force multiplier? It can yield outcomes beyond your expectations. Welcome to a better version of you and the road to personal fulfillment.

So, what did I just achieve with you? I introduce you to overlapping your mindset. It's better known as increasingly incongruent. With more common ground between self-image and ideal self, a person has greater self-worth and adopts a more positive frame of mind. If you fall off this path of being authentic, this is a barometer to get you back on track and keep you aligned with being your best self. To keep myself centered, I ask myself, "How do I see myself, rather than how do others see me."

When people's perception of who they are aligns with who they want to be, they achieve self-actualization. This realization of self satisfies the need to reach and express full potential. Carl Rogers made a compelling statement, " The good life is a process, not a state of being."

I close this chapter with this question for you. What if you complete the ending story of this question?

# Chapter Twenty-Four

# Hide-and-Seek

This may not apply to everyone, but I loved the game hide-and-seek as a kid. The joy of this game was beyond measure. I could play it for hours with my siblings or neighborhood friends. There was a time when playing outdoors was more fun than playing a game in the house. In addition, playing outside has multiple benefits. To name a few, the amount of exercise you get by playing outdoors, the absorption of natural vitamin D, and using your creative mind. Yes, these are the facts visually explained in my view.

The following statement I am about to make may come as a surprise. With that being said, we don't stop playing hide-and-seek when we're young. We keep playing this game far into adulthood, though the situation changes, and it's no longer fun. For example, when someone with an unresolved issue comes across our path unexpectedly, we try to move quickly, hoping they don't spot us. So, why do we try to hide from unresolved issues? More often than not, it's because of shame. We are ashamed of ourselves and don't want others to see what's happening with us. We frequently think people won't love us if they know who we are beyond the persona we portray.

The way to become a better version of yourself is to stop hiding. When you decide to come out from behind the bushes, you deal shame with a fatal blow. You must have the courage to confess that you are not perfect. It's time for you to break the code and forgive yourself for the past decisions you have made that were unfavorable.

Here's a compelling reason as to why you need to forgive yourself. Fifty percent of the stories we tell ourselves aren't even true. We must learn to break away from cultural thinking. It's leading us down a path we did not decide to take. It's almost as if everyone is trying to economize their thinking. So, what's my aim here?

I'm simply trying to remove you from an unconscious state of being into a conscious state of thinking. This process will not happen overnight, as many habits run deep. In addition, it takes sixty-six days to form a habit. Plus, you must prepare yourself for a new experience. If not, your mind will reject it as a new organ trying to enter your body. I encourage you to stay with me here, as you may be thinking about what this content has to do with leadership.

I say everything: we must begin to make better mind moves to have the right effect on people around us. If you are a leader, you are affecting not only your life but the life experiences of others. They're in the fishbowl with you. Our relationship with people can't be based on just the metrics but on our behavior of getting them to the metrics we seek.

Remember, your personality creates your reality. If you desire a new reality, you must change your personality. If you don't have the mind to do it, you will remain who you are. It's hard to teach your mind to make positive changes. Negative changes are easy. But why? They're based on habits, and habits don't require any thinking.

You can't become paralyzed by the pressure of delivering results. Many find themselves in this situation; it takes courage and faith to break out of this emotional state. You must try with every rudiment of your being to step out of fear and become a different leader. We have enough copycats out there and not enough originals.

There are 615 million people worldwide who suffer from anxiety or depression. Misguided emotions may be at the root of this worldwide epidemic. Good leaders see needs before the needs present themselves. Good leaders provide solutions, but great leaders invite others into the solution. Even if a leader can resolve the issue alone, there is value in having others participate in the action. They anticipate and prepare for problems before they happen.

Yes, there are people in your life who are addicted to negative emotions, and you won't be able to change that pleasure experience for them; it's their joy in life, so move on. However, thousands, if not millions, are seeking your embracing spirit. As leaders, people need us more than ever.

Humility happens when we leave our self-serving agendas to create the best opportunities for those around us. As a leader, you must learn to meet people where they are physically and emotionally. When people see your willingness to enter their world for the sake of the good, their productivity goes up exponentially.

The approximate number of hours a person will spend at work in a lifetime is 90,000. My question is, how many people's lives will you influence positively?

Part of your role as a leader should be making your organization great.

You have heard me use the term, "This may surprise you." With that said, these words should not surprise you. Promoting enthusiasm helps companies succeed, as employees must be motivated (both within themselves and by external rewards) to reach their goals. Companies have a role in creating a positive associate relations environment.

We place a lot on leaders as they are the gatekeepers in maintaining a healthy culture in the workplace. However, motivation is an internal state that drives a person to carry out particular behaviors or tasks. People are motivated by many things at work, including acquiring money, benefiting a social cause, and winning admiration. Employee motivation is directly correlated with job satisfaction and performance and indirectly with organizational success. In addition, if a company has a great career path process, employees are more likely to be motivated to perform well due to feeling their efforts will be rewarded.

If you, as a leader, get to a place where you're settling for "average," you need to reach out to someone who can help you reclaim your desire and inspiration to lead with vigor. You are never too old, weak, or broken to reflect positive change in others.

I encourage you to avoid the spirit of entitlement at all costs. This often happens when we feel a position is owed to us. We expect others to do the same if we believe we earned that position. It is the attitude of "I got mine, then you must earn yours." When, in fact, you honestly know that it was because of luck, hard work, grit, and timing.

No one is solely the success of their own doing.

I'm often reminded that no two people are alike. Each of us is uniquely created. With that, don't expect everyone to be like you. Encourage those under your leadership with inspiration and care. That's true power, not your title. Use your title to your advantage by becoming a servant leader. It is an honor to have a high position of power, but the challenge is how you use it. If you have an attitude of entitlement, you will seek ways to have people meet your needs. If you have a spirit of humbleness, you will use your position of power to create ways to serve others.

What I have shared with you was shared with me by numerous executive coaches who poured their knowledge into my life. I was never seeking for my work to be praiseworthy. However, I can only hope that I positively impacted someone's life.

We are more easily distracted by what's wrong with the world than the beauty around us. Our minds gravitate toward what's broken. Keep in mind that what we think about shapes what we see. If you constantly think about what could go wrong, you'll see the shortfalls of life and work.

I'm asking you to shift your focus and imagine what could be right. If you can achieve that, you will most likely see the goodness in others more clearly and experience more joy.

# Chapter Twenty-Five

# Co-Signing Silliness

This chapter is devoted to elevating common sense. We are often misguided by our emotions, leading us to make common errors in our decision-making. How many times have you found yourself saying these exact words? You know what's best for you but can't follow through. Engaging in behaviors and our inability to do the right thing can be frustrating. The question becomes, who will tell you what's correct or what you need to hear?

The truth of the matter is you may not be strong enough to overcome yourself. Habits run deep. So, it's not a surface extraction activity. In other words, you may be unable to change your actions. Your subconscious mind will not allow you to own your actions without following the proper steps.

Let's deal with the surface mind for just a minute. Some people will support your actions even if they know you are engaging in poor behaviors or wrong actions. I call this behavior co-signing silliness. We should never be enablers of actions that don't support honest and good behavior. Sadly, many people don't understand their actions.

This statement may sound contradictory to what you may have heard. I say stop trying to be your own hero. Confidence in self and the heart to be authentic embody good. Never turn your back on someone who may need your help.

The question becomes, why have so many people lost control of their focus and behavior? Perhaps we have been programmed to distraction and are unsure how to get back into flow or a conscious state of mind. It's okay because there is something heroic about knowing that we all have been fools at some point. It is the fool who speaks a truth nobody else dares to utter, and this brings instant relief because people know it has to be said. The fool may bring mental healing, but we must avoid being a professional fool.

How do you avoid being a professional fool? Follow your heart, not your mind.

There is no magic to getting your mind to mimic your heart. Being on autopilot is not just for airplanes; you see it daily when individuals engage in mindless activities while walking.

Even a clown must come out of uniform at some point. I remain optimistic that many minds will break out of senseless activity, return to what is considered normal, and engage in self-reflection.

When self-aware, we can alter misplaced emotions because we control the thoughts that cause them. In addition, self-observation profoundly changes the way we behave. Why? Most of our thoughts and actions are impulsive when we're not self-aware.

Allow me to slightly change the course and blow your mind. Some say pain is eternal, but suffering is optional.

What are the voices telling you?

Your probability of making the right choice is in a tiny window. So, what is your default mindset? Your default mindset is the vault you must unlock to see the truth.

I must be honest: in a few more decades, I'm unsure if we will be able to tell the difference between what is true and what is false as our perception of reality is shifting fast. Stay conscious of your feelings and in your heart, and you will most likely own your mind. If not, you will fall victim to believing everything you see and hear.

I consistently examine the labels I place on the things I see and hear. Remember, you are the air traffic controller of what goes in and out of your mind. This controlling part of the mind will not come easy. For example, we are getting increasingly distracted by the many data points and visual content we receive daily. We are all getting overloaded with too much information.

Do whatever it takes to redeem your thinking ability. It will require you to sacrifice many indulgences you depend on for joy or satisfaction.

I may have mentioned this before in a prior chapter. However, it's worth repeating. I had to give up watching TV and listening to the radio to regain my sanity. Now, I only read books and listen to classical music. My mind is very clear now that I have decided to commit to these two data points of content.

Also, be mindful of what stimulates you, as you may give rise to the wrong behaviors.

At the beginning of this chapter, I spoke about co-signing silliness and the people around you. With that, information can give you a point of release, knowing that someone else is partly responsible for your behavior. In fact, you may be the author of your lawless behavior. If that's the case, own it and make the mental pivot to be a better, authentic version of yourself and for those around you. I believe in you!

# Chapter Twenty-Six

# Walking off the Playground

Whether you are a non-profit or for-profit organization, it's essential that you discover a way to keep elements of fun in the workplace. You are partially correct if you think it's your organization's or executive team's responsibility to make it fun. However, just remember leadership is local, and your engagement with your customers and team is the true barometer of people's happiness with their environment. If you counter-argue that work should not be fun and everyone is paid to work to get the job done, I will challenge you by asking you to get your company data on retention and see how much it costs your company each year on recruiting and turnover. If another company can recruit your associate for $.50 or $.75 more in pay, you may have a playground opportunity.

Think about it: you have never seen a kid walk off the playground unless it was getting dark or recess time was up. When employees are happy, they don't leave for bribery. Research has shown that pay is not the only reason employees stay with their current employer.

I have been accused of repeating myself, so why stop now? Yes, I spoke about this in an earlier chapter, but if you missed the point, I'm putting it back in your face. It's just that vital to your business. I understand there's no policy for leaders to have these words exit their mouths, such as, please, thank you, I appreciate you, and how's your family doing. However, I can assure you those words will go far beyond any monetary pay, not to mention the effect they have on morale in the workplace. This single activity alone can create a positive associate relations environment within any company. If you are a startup company or existing business looking to create a positive and motivating environment, here are some strategies to consider:

- **Clear Vision and Values:** Communicate a compelling mission and values that resonate with associates. Make them feel that they are part of something meaningful.

- **Recognition and Appreciation:** Regularly acknowledge and celebrate associates' hard work and achievements. Recognize both individual and team contributions.

- **Inclusive Culture:** Foster an inclusive workplace where diversity is valued and everyone feels heard and respected. Inclusion can boost pride and a sense of belonging.

- **Training and Development:** Invest in continuous learning and development opportunities. Offer training that helps associates grow in their roles and advance their careers.

- **Empowerment:** Give associates more autonomy and decision-making power within their roles. Feeling trusted and empowered can boost pride and ownership.

- **Career Progression:** Create clear paths for career advancement within the company. When associates see growth opportunities, they are more likely to take pride in their work.

- **Feedback Mechanisms:** Implement regular feedback mechanisms to collect input from associates. Act on their suggestions and involve them in decision-making when possible.

- **Safe and Healthy Environment:** Prioritize the physical and mental well-being of associates. Ensure a safe, clean, and comfortable workplace.

- **Team Building:** Encourage team-building activities to build strong bonds among associates. A cohesive team often takes pride in their collective accomplishments.

- **Customer-Centric Focus:** Emphasize the importance of exceptional customer service. When associates see their positive impact on customers, it can boost their pride in their work.

- **Community Engagement:** Engage in community initiatives or charity work that associates can participate in. It can give them a sense of pride in contributing to a greater cause.

- **Transparency and Communication:** Keep associates informed about company goals, performance, and changes. Transparency can create a sense of ownership and pride.

- **Employee Benefits:** Offer competitive compensation and benefits packages. Feeling well-compensated and supported financially can contribute to pride in the workplace.

- **Sustainability Initiatives:** If the company is involved in sustainability efforts, associates should be involved. Many employees take pride in working for environmentally responsible organizations.

- **Lead by Example:** Leadership should exemplify the values and behaviors expected from associates. When leaders take pride in their work, it can inspire others to do the same.

By implementing these strategies, retail leaders can help associates take pride in their work, feel valued, and be more engaged, improving job satisfaction and performance.

# Chapter Twenty-Seven

# I'm in My Right Mind

As a kid growing up, I used to hear older adults use the words "I'm in my right mind" when someone would ask them how they were doing. As a kid, I used to wonder why they would say those words and what they meant by saying those words. Perhaps it was a Southern folklore term. As a young boy, I thought everyone was in their right mind. However, as I grew older, this statement took on a new meaning, and I developed a deep admiration for those words.

I'm amazed by the simple things we take for granted when unaware. To them, if they woke up and were able to remember what day of the week it was and the name of the person that was greeting them, plus they were mentally in a peaceful place, they considered it to be a blessed day knowing that they were in their conscious mind. Here's the unspoken wisdom they also possessed: They knew that many individuals were grappling with fear and anger and consumed with too much pride.

Life only cares about the content of our attention, and those three words drive 90 percent of our actions. You can mobilize a mass group just by focusing on those three words. You may be thinking if you are of a certain age, your mind is fully functional and alert. You're in great mental standing. But are you?

Most of our decisions are made unconsciously. So, are you really in your right mind at all times?

Here's a proven way to give you the best chance at making sound decisions. You must control your perceptions because everything we hear is an opinion, not a fact, and everything we see is our perspective, not the truth. There is so much waste of information going through our eyes and ears that it's hard for anyone to collectively take in quality quantitative information.

Allow me to provide you with some simple activities you can engage in with a degree of certainty that it can provide you with proven results. If appropriately executed, these activities can reduce your learning time and enhance your mental and cognitive skills. They are:

- **Active Learning:** Instead of passively consuming information, engage actively with the material. Take notes, ask questions, and discuss topics with others to deepen your understanding.

- **Chunking:** Break down complex information into smaller, manageable chunks. Focus on mastering chunks at a time before moving on to the next.

- **Space Repetition:** Review and revise information periodically over time. This technique helps improve long-term retention.

- **Mind Mapping:** Create visual representations of concepts and ideas using mind maps. This can help you organize and recall information more effectively.

- **Speed Reading:** Practice speed reading techniques to increase reading speed while maintaining comprehension.

- **Teaching Others:** Teaching what you've learned to someone else reinforces your understanding and helps identify gaps in your knowledge.

- **Healthy Lifestyle:** Prioritize physical health through regular exercise, a balanced diet, and adequate sleep. A healthy body supports cognitive function.

- **Learn a New Skill:** Challenge yourself by learning a new language, musical instrument, or skill. This promotes neural plasticity and cognitive growth.

- **Goal Setting:** Set clear learning goals and objectives. Having a specific target can motivate and focus your efforts.

- **Feedback:** Seek feedback from mentors, peers, or instructors. Constructive criticism can help you identify areas for improvement.

- **Continuous Learning:** Cultivate a growth mindset and embrace a lifelong learning mentality. Be open to new ideas and knowledge.

- **Limit Distractions:** Create a conducive learning environment by minimizing distractions and practicing focused attention.

- **Rest and Recovery:** Allow time for breaks and relaxation to prevent burnout and maintain mental freshness.

I talked about controlling your perceptions at the top of this chapter, with the understanding that everything we see and hear is not a fact but rather an opinion. With that said, here's the most critical part of this chronological path to controlling our perceptions: monitoring our thoughts.

Monitoring our thoughts before rendering a verdict on our decisions is critical for several reasons, particularly in the context of Vedanta philosophy and many other philosophical and ethical traditions:

- **Clarity and Wisdom:** Vedanta emphasizes the importance of clarity and wisdom in decision-making. By monitoring our thoughts, we ensure impulsive reactions or biases do not cloud our judgments.

- **Self-Reflection:** Vedanta encourages self-reflection and self-awareness. Monitoring our thoughts allows us to examine our underlying beliefs, desires, and motivations, helping us make decisions that align with our true values and principles.

- **Reducing Impulsivity:** Impulsive decisions can lead to regrets. Monitoring our thoughts provide actions, allowing us to pause, reflect, and make more considered choices.

- **Avoiding Negative Consequences:** Negative thoughts, such as anger, envy, or greed, can lead to unwise decisions. We can avoid actions that may harm ourselves or others by monitoring and addressing these negative thoughts.

- **Emotional Balance:** Vedanta promotes emotional balance and equanimity. By monitoring our thoughts, we can manage emotional reactions and ensure that decisions are made from a place of inner calm and balance.

- **Responsible Decision-Making:** In the broader context of life and society, monitoring thoughts helps ensure responsible decision-making that respects the rights and well-being of others.

In summary, monitoring our thoughts before rendering a verdict on our decisions is a foundational practice in Vedanta and many other philosophical and ethical traditions. It promotes self-awareness, wisdom, ethical conduct, and alignment with higher principles, ultimately leading to more mindful and meaningful decision-making.

Remember that everyone's learning pace and cognitive abilities vary. The key is to find a combination of techniques and strategies that work best for you and align with your learning goals. Consistency and dedication are crucial in collapsing learning time and enhancing cognitive skills. Yes, it's time for you to recalibrate.

# Chapter Twenty-Eight

# I Want It All

Goal setting is fading in the workplace, and more people have settled with just getting by or barely surviving. Most of this lack of drive is caused by what's happening in the world and the economy. So, what is this telling us? Things happening at a distance have the same effect as if we were dealing with the matter firsthand. With that said, unbeknownst to all of us, we have been experiencing telepathy for many years prior. Another way of putting it is that we have been projecting our emotions on others without their permission. If I cry, you cry; if I smile, you smile, and I don't have to know or have a relationship with you. Emotions are contagious; you can transmit your feelings to others in a different state or country. You may be asking, what does this contagious activity have to do with you or the workplace?

It's another way of gradually describing the behaviors of deception. When things are moving at a pace undetected to the human eye, it's natural for us to tell ourselves nothing is taking place because we can't see it from a visual standpoint.

You may have lost your drive to excel or set goals for yourself, which has nothing to do with what you are going through or experiencing on the job. It could be as simple as the vibe in the building or store you work in.

I have witnessed individuals with high intellect and potential settle for average results.

Check this out: a person does not have to have dialogue with you for you to catch their emotions.

Allow me to provide you with a very simple reminder to help you stay on track for setting and achieving your goals regardless of the environment. As a child, do you remember your parents saying, "That's not how we do it in this family?" They wanted you to know that your family's standards differ from those you saw around you.

In my case, my mother was a single parent, and when people in the neighborhood saw me get out of line, they would remind me that that's not how my mother raised me. More importantly, I did not want to let my mother down. Adults in my neighborhood reminded me of my identity as a child of Claudette. I was held to a greater standard of behavior once I heard those words. This became a significant source of my goal-setting in work and life.

You must be aware of the subtle shift in your perspective because despair is minutes away from taking residence in your mind, and getting an eviction for despair is not an easy extraction.

Allow me to put this disclaimer out there: I am not a trained psychologist in any way, shape, or form. However, I will give you my advice as a leader to help others deal with elements of despair:

- **Be an active listener:** As leaders, we must remain active listeners, encouraging our associates and subordinates to discuss their feelings and concerns. Sometimes, simply being heard and understood can provide relief.

- **Help individuals set small, achievable goals:** Accomplishing even small tasks can provide a sense of purpose and progress.

- **Encourage self-care:** Stress the importance of self-care routines, including exercise, healthy eating, and getting enough sleep. Physical well-being can significantly impact mental health.

- **Engage in volunteer work:** Suggest volunteering or helping others in need. Acts of kindness can boost one's sense of purpose and fulfillment.

- **Limit News Consumption:** Excessive exposure to negative news can contribute to despair. Encourage them to limit news consumption and focus on positive or educational content.

- **Gratitude journaling:** I recommend keeping a gratitude journal to help recognize and appreciate the positive aspects of life, no matter how small. Writing this book is therapy for me.

- **Creative outlets:** Encourage creative hobbies or activities, such as art, writing, or music, which can serve as emotional outlets and sources of joy. My other outlet is yard work. It's my other form of therapy; working in my yard is pleasing and relaxing.

- **Professional development:** Explore opportunities for skill development or career growth that align with their interests and aspirations.

- **Nature and outdoors:** Spending time in nature or the outdoors can have a calming and rejuvenating effect. Encourage activities like hiking or simply taking a walk in the park.

- **Set boundaries:** Help them establish healthy relationships and work-life boundaries to prevent burnout and emotional exhaustion.

- **Celebrate small wins:** Celebrate any small achievements or moments of happiness along the way. Recognizing progress, no matter how minor, can be motivating.

We can have it all. And that's a balanced life! But we must rid ourselves of the mentality that we are perfect and embrace that we aren't the superhero we sometimes believe we need to be. It's time we realize that we lead best when we allow ourselves to be imperfect.

Do to others what you would want them to do to you. You should have learned this simple behavior in preschool, as it was taught worldwide. This lesson is no less true in our homes, businesses, and lives. Do to others what you want done to you. My question to you as a leader is, are you modeling the behavior you want to see in those you have authority over? It's easy to lead out of power and fear, but the best way for us to lead is through treating others the way we wish to be treated.

# Chapter Twenty-Nine

# The Mirage of Control

In today's fast-paced world, the illusion that we're in control of every situation has become a prevalent mindset. We create these self-made castles in our minds where we think we're the kings and queens, ruling over our emotions, decisions, and actions. But here's a reality check: are you really in control? The answer is not as simple as yes or no. Your decisions, believe it or not, are often influenced by external factors you haven't even considered. I call this the mirage of control.

Let's dig deeper into this. You wake up every day, go to work, make decisions, come back home, and the cycle repeats. You think you are making all these decisions, but how much of it is really you? Your environment, the people around you, and the culture you're part of all have a role in this mirage. Your subconscious mind picks up cues, and before you even realize it, your conscious mind executes actions based on them.

So, what's the big deal, you ask? Well, understanding that you may not be entirely in control can be both liberating and frightening. It is liberating because you realize the limitations of human nature and frightening because it puts you on a path of self-questioning. It's a double-edged sword, but one worth wielding if you aim to be a true leader.

Leaders don't just navigate their emotions and decisions; they're responsible for influencing others. So, if you're under the illusion that you're in complete control, you're deceiving yourself and those who look up to you. The key to breaking this mirage is awareness. Once you become aware of the external factors that influence you, you can better control your actions and, by extension, the actions of those around you.

This is not to say you should be paranoid and start questioning every single decision or thought. That way lies madness. But a little bit of introspection has never harmed anyone. In fact, it should be a regular exercise, especially if you're in a leadership role.

Why does all this matter? Because the world we live in is not static. It's dynamic, changing every single moment. If you're stuck in the mirage of control, you'll be ill-equipped to adapt to these changes. Adaptation is the cornerstone of survival, not just in the biological sense but also in business and personal relationships.

In my previous chapters, I've talked about co-signing silliness, elevating common sense, and the deception of the gradual. All these themes converge to this point. Leadership isn't just about managing people or making big decisions; it's about understanding human nature, starting with your own.

So, take a step back, reflect on your actions, understand the influence of the environment and people around you, and then make informed decisions. This doesn't mean you'll achieve absolute control, but you'll be closer to understanding the dynamics that influence it. And in that understanding, you'll find authentic leadership.

I'll leave you with this thought: control is not about having a grip on everything; it's about understanding what you can grip and what you should let go. Navigate wisely.

# Chapter Thirty

# The Mind-Numbing Effects of Technology in Leadership

A Great Tool or an Evil Process?

We live in an increasingly digital world where technology has permeated every facet of our lives. Technology is an ever-present force, from the smartphones in our pockets to the algorithms that dictate our online experiences. But while technology offers unprecedented advantages, it also presents unique challenges, especially in the realm of leadership. I call this the dual nature of technology in leadership. It can either be an excellent tool for empowerment or a process that numbs the mind and dilutes genuine leadership qualities.

Let's start with the positives. Technology has democratized information, allowing for greater transparency and quicker decision-making processes. Communication tools have made it easier for leaders to stay in touch with their teams, regardless of geographic location. Data analytics can provide real-time insights into market trends, customer behavior, and organizational performance. These tools can make you a more effective, insightful leader. They can amplify your reach, fine-tune your strategies, and offer you perspectives that were unthinkable a few decades ago.

But here's the rub: while technology can amplify good leadership qualities, it can equally magnify poor ones. If you depend too much on digital communication, you risk losing the personal touch essential in leadership. Rely solely on data analytics, and you could overlook the nuances that aren't easily quantifiable. Worse yet, the overuse of technology can lead to decision-making paralysis—the overreliance on data and tools at the expense of gut instinct and human judgment.

Furthermore, technology can be incredibly distracting. The constant bombardment of notifications, messages, and updates can fracture your attention, making it difficult to focus on tasks that require deep thought and concentration. We are always connected, always reachable, and that's not necessarily a good thing. This perpetual state of "connectedness" can lead to mental fatigue, reducing your effectiveness as a leader.

Now, let's talk about the darker aspects of technology. Algorithms are designed to show us content we will likely engage with, creating echo chambers that reinforce our existing beliefs and viewpoints. This is a dangerous prospect for any leader. A good leader listens to differing opinions, considers all sides of an argument, and is willing to change their mind when presented with new information. Technology, if not carefully managed, can close off these avenues and entrench our existing beliefs.

Social media presents its own set of challenges. While it can be a powerful tool for branding and outreach, it's also rife with pitfalls. A poorly thought-out tweet or an insensitive post can quickly spiral out of control, causing significant damage to your reputation. In today's cancel culture, the stakes are incredibly high.

So, what's the solution? Abandon technology and go back to the dark ages? Of course not. The key is mindful usage. Understand the limitations of technology and use it as a tool, not a crutch. Use data analytics to inform your decisions, but don't ignore your instincts. Use digital communication tools to supplement, but not replace, face-to-face interactions. Be aware of the echo chambers that can form around you, and make a conscious effort to break free from them.

Leadership in the digital age requires a delicate balancing act. On one hand, you have access to tools and information that can make you incredibly effective. On the other hand, the overreliance on these tools can make you disconnected, less effective, and even less human.

In the previous chapters, we've explored various facets of leadership, from the mirage of control to co-signing silliness. This chapter serves as a cautionary tale but also as a guide. Technology is a double-edged sword. Wield it wisely, and it can cut through the complexities of modern leadership, empowering you to lead more effectively than ever before. But wield it recklessly, and it can turn against you, numbing your mind and diluting your leadership qualities.

In conclusion, technology is neither good nor bad; its value is determined by how we use it. As we navigate this digital landscape, let's consciously use technology to enhance, rather than diminish, our leadership abilities. Remember, technology should be your servant, not your master.

# Chapter Thirty-One

# Starting at the Bottom

We often hear rags-to-riches stories in business, tales of individuals who started at the bottom of the corporate ladder and worked up to supervisory or managerial roles. These stories are inspiring and compelling, serving as a testament to the idea that hard work and perseverance can lead to success. But let's dig a little deeper. Does starting from the bottom and working your way up necessarily make you a good leader? Data suggests otherwise.

Starting at the bottom has its advantages. It allows you to understand the company's fundamental operations, appreciate frontline employees' challenges, and establish rapport with staff at all levels. These experiences can provide invaluable insights when moving into a leadership role.

However, the transition from an individual contributor to a leader is fraught with challenges. One of the most common pitfalls is the lack of proper training and support. Most companies focus on technical and operational efficiency but neglect the soft skills required for effective leadership. Leadership isn't just about being good at your job; it's about inspiring and motivating others to be good at theirs.

Another significant issue is that climbing the corporate ladder often cultivates a mindset focused on individual achievement rather than team success. When such individuals become leaders, they may lack the collaborative skills necessary to manage a team effectively. They might be more concerned about their career progression than their team members' growth and well-being. The disconnect is evident when these new leaders struggle to motivate their teams.

Motivation is a complex psychological process, and what drives one person may not necessarily drive another. A good leader understands these nuances and knows how to tap into individual strengths to inspire collective achievement. However, if you've never been trained in these aspects of leadership, you're essentially sailing a ship without a compass.

So, what's the solution? The key is comprehensive leadership training that goes beyond just operational skills. Companies must invest in programs that teach emotional intelligence, conflict resolution, and the art of motivation. Moreover, mentorship should be encouraged. Learning from someone who has been there and done that can offer insights that no textbook can provide.

To sum up, starting at the bottom and working your way up can offer invaluable operational insights, but it's not enough to make you a good leader. Proper training and support are crucial in transitioning from an individual contributor to a leader who can motivate and inspire teams. It's not just about climbing the ladder; it's about learning to keep everyone balanced as you ascend.

# Chapter Thirty-Two

# Starting at the Bottom (Cont'd)

Addressing another facet of this issue is imperative: how companies can remedy this leadership gap. The solution isn't a one-size-fits-all approach; it's a multi-tiered strategy involving upper management, human resources, and emerging leaders.

Firstly, companies must integrate leadership training into their employee development programs. This training shouldn't just be a cursory two-day workshop but an ongoing program that includes real-world simulations, case studies, and mentorship. This can help prepare individuals for the multifaceted challenges they will face as leaders.

Secondly, mentorship programs can serve as a bridge between theoretical knowledge and practical application. Pairing emerging leaders with experienced ones can give them a platform to discuss challenges, strategize solutions, and, most importantly, learn from failures.

Lastly, self-awareness should be at the forefront of these training programs. Emerging leaders must understand their leadership styles, strengths, weaknesses, and how they impact those around them. Psychometric tests, 360-degree feedback, and regular performance reviews can provide valuable insights into these areas.

# Chapter Thirty-Three

# A Square Peg in a Round Hole: Leading the 21st Century Employee Frontier

The 21st century heralds an era of unprecedented transformation. As technology reshapes industries and globalization redraws boundaries, the workforce undergoes a significant metamorphosis. Today's employees are defined not just by their roles but by their aspirations, values, and the unique blend of skills they bring to the table. It begs the question: are our current leaders equipped to guide this new frontier of employees, or are they trying to fit a square peg into a round hole?

Traditionally, organizations functioned like well-oiled machines. Each component, or in this case, each employee, had a defined role. There was a clear hierarchy, a set path for growth, and uniformity in expectations. However, the digital revolution changed that. Today's employees are more like nodes in a vast, interconnected, interdependent, and incredibly diverse network.

This diversity is not just in demographics but also in thought, ambition, and approach to work. Having grown up in a digitally connected world, the Millennial and Gen Z workforce values flexibility, purpose, and collaborative environments. They are less motivated by the traditional carrot-and-stick approach and more by a sense of purpose and the potential for personal and professional growth.

So, how do leaders, many of whom were groomed in the 20th-century paradigm, adapt to this shift? How do they ensure that they are not just fitting square pegs into round holes but reshaping them to accommodate the diverse pegs? The first step is recognition. Leaders must acknowledge that the rules of the game have changed. Hierarchical structures might need to give way to more flexible, team-based approaches. Feedback loops need to be shorter, and decision-making needs to be more collaborative. The one-size-fits-all approach to leadership is obsolete.

Next comes empathy. The 21st-century employee seeks validation, not just for their work but for their unique perspective. Leaders must learn to listen actively, understand the motivations of their team members, and provide a platform where they feel valued. But it's not all about adaptability. Leaders also have a responsibility to guide and mentor. The vast ocean of information available today can often be overwhelming. The role of a leader is to help their team navigate these waters, identify the right opportunities, and grow both personally and professionally.

Now, imagine a world where leaders are no longer just commanders but collaborators—a world where leadership is not defined by the number of orders given but by the number of hands raised for innovative ideas. That's the world of the 21st century employee frontier. It's a world where the round holes are flexible, accommodating not just the square pegs but also the triangular, hexagonal, and octagonal ones.

In conclusion, as the lines between work and life blur, aspirations become as crucial as salaries, and collaboration overshadows command, leadership needs a new definition. The 21st-century leader is a guide and fellow traveler, exploring the vast frontier of possibilities alongside their team. And as they journey together, they create a landscape that's inclusive, dynamic, and ripe with potential.

# Chapter Thirty-Four

# Navigating the Generational Jungle: A Leader's Hilariously Twisted Guide

Alright, leaders, buckle up! We're embarking on a rollercoaster ride through the wild and wacky world of the multi-generational workforce. Picture this: a workplace where Baby Boomers are trying to explain vinyl records to Gen Zers, who can't even fathom a world without Wi-Fi. Meanwhile, Millennials are in the corner, snapping selfies and sipping on their almond milk lattes, while Gen Xers are just shaking their heads, nostalgic about the 'good old days' of dial-up internet. It's like a sitcom, only this time, you're the star!

First off, let's talk about the Baby Boomers. Ah, the generation that walked five miles uphill (both ways!) to school. They've seen it all, from black and white TV to the marvels of virtual reality. And while they might occasionally struggle to differentiate between a tweet and a chirp, their work ethic is unparalleled. Pro tip: If you want to get on their good side, just throw in a reference to the Beatles or rotary phones.

Next up, the Gen Xers. Sandwiched between the idealistic Boomers and the tech-savvy Millennials, these are the folks who remember life before Google. They've mastered the art of the eye roll, especially when someone says, "There's an app for that." But don't be fooled; they're the glue holding the generational puzzle together. They're as comfortable with a typewriter as a tablet, making them the ultimate generational chameleon.

Enter the Millennials. Ah, the avocado toast-loving, wanderlust-chasing dreamers. They might have ten different side hustles and a penchant for yoga, but they're also the pioneers of the digital age. They've redefined the traditional 9-to-5 and are on a mission to find purpose in everything they do. And if they can snap a picture for Instagram along the way, even better!

Last but not least, Gen Z. These digital dynamos were practically born with smartphones in their hands. They're entrepreneurial, socially conscious, and have a meme for every occasion. And while they might communicate in emojis and TikTok dances, their passion and creativity know no bounds.

So, how does a leader juggle this motley crew? With a sense of humor, of course! Create a 'Decade Day' where everyone dresses up from their favorite era. Organize a 'Tech Swap' workshop where Boomers share tales of the legendary fax machine, and Gen Zers introduce them to the wonders of Snapchat. Encourage cross-generational coffee breaks, and watch as hilarity ensues.

In all seriousness (well, kind of), leading a multi-generational team is like hosting a family dinner. There's the wise grandparent, the rebellious teen, the know-it-all uncle, and the enthusiastic kid. And while there might be some eye-rolling and playful banter, they all share the same table at the end of the day.

In conclusion, embrace the chaos, celebrate the differences, and always keep a sense of humor. After all, laughter is the universal language that transcends all generations. And who knows?

You might just learn a thing or two along the way.

# Chapter Thirty-Five

# Building Bridges, Not Walls

You've heard this before, but it bears repeating: open lines of communication are critical. But it's not just about talking; it's about listening too. Let's say a Boomer is waxing poetic: "Back in my day, we had face-to-face meetings, not these Zoom calls!" Instead of dismissing this as archaic, use it as an opportunity. Organize monthly in-person roundtables or "Old School Office Hours," where team members can discuss ideas without digital distractions. In turn, let Gen Zers run a "Social Media Savvy" seminar to keep the older generations in the loop on the latest platforms.

## The Language of Appreciation

Each generation has a different communication style and different expectations for recognition. Boomers may appreciate a formal, written acknowledgment, while Millennials might prefer a shoutout on the company Slack channel. Gen Xers, often the skeptics, may value straightforward, no-frills feedback, while Gen Zers love public recognition but in a digital format, like an Instagram story celebrating their achievements. Take the time to learn how each generation likes to be appreciated.

## Leveraging Skills and Experience

Baby Boomers have a wealth of experience, but they can often feel overshadowed by younger generations more proficient with technology. Use their experience wisely.

Create mentorship programs pairing Boomers with younger employees. Likewise, encourage Millennials and Gen Zers to offer 'Tech Tuesdays,' where they can impart digital wisdom to their older coworkers.

## Flexibility is Your Friend

Gen Xers and Millennials value work-life balance and often seek flexible work arrangements. Recognize this and offer remote work options or flexible hours if possible. It will not only boost morale but also introduce older generations to new ways of working that they may not have considered.

## The Great Unifier: Purpose

As different as these generations are, they all seek a sense of purpose in their work. Whether it's the Baby Boomers who were part of the civil rights and anti-war movements or the Gen Zers fervently advocating for climate change action, people want to feel like they are part of something bigger than themselves. Make it a point to regularly communicate the company's mission and how each team member contributes to it.

## A Culture of Continuous Learning

Make ongoing education a cornerstone of your company culture. Whether a Gen Xer learns about sustainability from a Gen Z coworker or a Millennial picking up negotiation tips from a Boomer, encourage cross-generational knowledge sharing. You could even host a 'Generational Talent Show,' where each group teaches the others a valuable skill or knowledge.

## The Power of Empathy

Lastly, but perhaps most importantly, cultivate empathy. Create an environment where everyone feels their voice is heard, their skills are utilized, and their value is recognized- regardless of their generation.

In the final analysis, navigating the multi-generational workforce isn't just about mitigating conflict; it's about fostering an inclusive, dynamic environment where the sum is greater than its individual parts. Because, in the end, it's not just about surviving this generational jungle; it's about thriving in it.

As I wrap up this chapter, I hope you've found some actionable tips and perhaps even a chuckle or two. Remember, leading a diverse team may have challenges, but the rewards are immeasurable. So go ahead and embrace the chaos, celebrate the quirks, and lead with empathy and humor. After all, what's a jungle without a bit of laughter?

# Chapter Thirty-Six

# Embracing Emotions: Leading Beyond the Numbers

In the fast-paced world of spreadsheets, analytics, and key performance indicators, it's easy to overlook one of the most critical aspects of leadership: emotional intelligence. This chapter delves into the crucial role emotions play in team dynamics, particularly in a multigenerational workplace. We're shifting our focus from metrics to something less quantifiable but equally vital: the human element.

## The Emotional Landscape of a Multi-Generational Team

The first thing to understand is that each generation has a unique emotional landscape shaped by their formative years' events, technologies, and cultural shifts. Baby Boomers, often driven by loyalty and a strong work ethic, may find emotional satisfaction in long-term company commitment and incremental progress. Millennials and Gen Z, on the other hand, are often driven by a sense of immediate purpose and social impact, which translates to a need for frequent emotional boosts and validation.

As a leader, it's your job to recognize these nuanced emotional needs and find a middle ground. Create an environment where everyone feels emotionally secure and valued regardless of their generational background. One way to do this is through "Emotionally Intelligent Meetings," where, aside from project updates, team members can share personal victories or challenges they are facing. The aim is to create a platform for emotional expression and empathy, transcending generational gaps.

## Emotional Capital: The Unseen Currency

We often talk about human capital skills, talents, and the ability to perform tasks. However, emotional capital, the reservoir of goodwill and positive feelings among team members is just emotional needs that play a significant role in their job satisfaction and performance. By embracing emotions and leading with emotional intelligence, you can navigate the complexities of a multi-generational team with finesse and empathy. After all, metrics may fill spreadsheets, but emotions fill a workplace with life, making it a vibrant ecosystem where everyone thrives.

This is where your emotional intelligence comes into play. Reading the room, understanding unspoken tensions, and resolving conflicts diplomatically can turn a group of individual contributors into a cohesive, high-performing team.

Building emotional capital requires consistent effort. Simple gestures like acknowledging birthdays, celebrating personal milestones, or *even* a spontaneous "good job" can go a long way. These actions might seem small, but they accumulate, creating an emotional bank you can draw from in times of conflict or stress.

## The ROI of Emotional Intelligence

Investing in emotional intelligence has tangible returns. An emotionally connected team is likelier to be engaged, creative, and committed to collective goals. In a multi generational setting, this is crucial for bridging the gap between different work ethics, communication styles, and expectations.

How do you measure this ROI? Look beyond the usual metrics. Pay attention to team morale, the quality of interpersonal relationships, and the level of enthusiasm during meetings. These soft indicators often precede hard results like increased productivity or improved customer satisfaction ratings.

In summary, leading beyond the numbers means acknowledging that your team is more than

# Chapter Thirty-Seven

# The Emotional Toolbox: Practical Strategies for a Harmonious Multi-Generational Workplace

Emotional intelligence is not just a buzzword; it's a crucial skill set for any leader aiming to manage a multi-generational team effectively. Having established the importance of emotional intelligence in the previous chapter, let's now pivot to the "how." How can you, as a leader, implement emotional intelligence in practical, everyday scenarios? This chapter outlines actionable strategies to equip you with an "emotional toolbox" for leading your diverse team.

## Emotional Literacy: The Foundation of Understanding

The first tool in your emotional toolbox should be emotional literacy—the ability to recognize, understand, and appropriately express emotions. Just as you wouldn't ignore key financial metrics, don't neglect the emotional pulse of your team. Conduct regular one-on-ones, not just to discuss tasks and performance but also to check in emotionally. Ask open-ended questions like, "How are you feeling about the current project?" or "Is there anything you're struggling with that you'd like to discuss?"

In a multi-generational context, emotional literacy also means understanding generational nuances in emotional expression. Baby Boomers may be more reserved and less likely to openly discuss work-related stress, while Millennials and Gen Z might be more open about their emotional state. Adapt your approach to suit these generational differences.

## Active Listening: The Bridge to Empathy

Active listening is more than just hearing; it's about understanding the underlying emotions and motives behind the words. When a Gen Xer says, "I miss the days when we used to collaborate in the office," they might be expressing a more profound feeling of isolation or a craving for direct interaction. Similarly, when a Millennial proposes more remote working days, they might be seeking a better work-life balance to address burnout.

Active listening also involves body language and tone. For instance, if a Baby Boomer seems hesitant while discussing a new tech tool, they might feel overwhelmed but are too proud to admit it. In such cases, training sessions should be offered to ease the transition, addressing the emotional concern without making it a point of contention.

## Emotional Regulation: The Art of Balance

Emotional regulation isn't about suppressing emotions; it's about managing them constructively. As the leader, you set the emotional tone for the team. Your ability to maintain emotional balance during high-stress situations can significantly impact team morale.

For example, guide the team toward constructive problem-solving instead of focusing on blame during a project setback. Use phrases like, "Let's figure this out together" or "Mistakes happen; what's important is how we move forward." This approach reduces stress and fosters a culture of collective responsibility and resilience.

In a multi-generational team, emotional regulation is even more critical. The younger generation might look to you for cues on handling stress and setbacks. In comparison, the older generation might see your emotional stability as a sign of maturity and leadership competence.

## Conflict Resolution: The Emotional Fire Extinguisher

Conflict is inevitable in any team, but even more so in a multi-generational one, where differences in communication styles, work ethics, and expectations can lead to misunderstandings. Here's where your emotional toolbox can be a lifesaver.

When conflicts arise, address them promptly but tactfully. Use "I" statements to avoid sounding accusatory, such as "I've noticed some tension during our meetings, and I'd like to understand how everyone is feeling so we can resolve it." Allow each party to express their views and validate their emotions without necessarily agreeing with their point.

## Emotional Investment: The Long-Term Strategy

Lastly, remember that emotional intelligence is not a one-off initiative but a long-term investment. Regularly update your emotional toolbox. Keep abreast of new research on emotional intelligence and generational dynamics. You could even consider bringing in an emotional intelligence consultant for specialized training sessions, focusing on how each generation can learn to better understand the others.

The long-term benefits of this emotional investment are manifold. Not only will you see an improvement in team collaboration and productivity, but you'll also notice a more positive workplace culture marked by mutual respect and understanding among all generations.

As you navigate the labyrinthine complexities of leading a multi-generational team, your emotional toolbox will guide you through interpersonal dynamics and conflicts. While spreadsheets and performance metrics are essential, they're only one part of the equation. Emotional intelligence fills the other half, offering a more holistic view of leadership, considering the full spectrum of human experience.

Remember, a multi-generational team is not just a challenge; it's an opportunity to blend the wisdom of experience with the innovation of youth, guided by the empathetic leadership that respects and values both. So, as you lead your team into the future, ensure you're equipped with an emotional toolbox that's as diverse and versatile as your team. Because at the end of the day, it's not just about meeting targets; it's about meeting hearts.

# Chapter Thirty-Eight

## "The Power of Paradox: Embracing Contradictions in Leadership"

In a world fraught with complexity, today's leaders often find themselves navigating a maze of paradoxes. On the one hand, they're encouraged to be decisive; on the other, they're told to be open-minded. They're asked to be compassionate yet firm, innovative yet rooted in tradition, global outlook, and yet local approach. It's like being a Swiss Army knife in human form, with a tool for every occasion.

Welcome to the paradoxical world of leadership, where contradictions aren't just inevitable; they're instrumental to success.

Now, let's take a step back and chuckle at the image of a Swiss Army knife with a business suit and a briefcase, presenting quarterly reports in a boardroom. Hilarious, isn't it? Well, you might not be too far off. Today's business leaders need a diverse skill set, akin to that multi-tool pocket wonder, to navigate the ever-changing business landscape.

## The Decisive Open Mind

In the fast-paced environment of the business world, leaders often have to make split-second decisions. They are expected to cut through the noise and make choices that can make or break their companies. However, this decisiveness should not come at the expense of open-mindedness.

The most effective leaders are those who can decisively act while keeping an open mind for alternative solutions and perspectives. It's like being a chef specializing in Italian cuisine but is open to adding a dash of Japanese wasabi to spice up a traditional pasta dish. The result might be extraordinary, a delightful fusion that appeals to diverse palates. And isn't that what business innovation is all about?

## Compassionate Firmness

Let's get real for a second; leading people is not a walk in the park. You're not herding sheep; you're guiding a group of diverse, opinionated, and often strong-willed individuals. It's like trying to conduct an orchestra where every musician thinks they're the star of the show.

Leaders need to strike a balance between compassion and firmness. Compassion ensures employees feel valued and understood, fostering a positive work environment. Firmness, on the other hand, ensures that deadlines are met and quality is maintained. It's like being a parent who knows when to offer a comforting hug and when to lay down the law. You're essentially the good cop and the bad cop, all rolled into one.

Balancing Innovation and Tradition

# Chapter Thirty-Nine

# Confidence, an Underutilized Co-pilot

Confidence is an essential element of success, often serving as an underutilized co-pilot on the journey toward achieving your goals. It's a quality that manifests differently in everyone, yet its presence is universally recognized and respected. In this chapter, we delve into the intricate relationship between confidence and success, illustrated through the lives and philosophies of Elon Musk, Warren Buffet, and Bill Gates.

## Elon Musk: The Audacity of Ambition

Elon Musk, the CEO of SpaceX and Tesla, is a paragon of audacious confidence. His ventures into space exploration, electric vehicles, and even tunnel construction are fueled by a level of self-assurance that most would find intimidating. He once said, "When something is important enough, you do it even if the odds are not in your favor."

This statement encapsulates the essence of Musk's confidence. He doesn't merely play the odds; he challenges them, reshaping entire industries in the process. This kind of confidence doesn't come from arrogance but from a deeply rooted belief in one's abilities and the courage to act upon it.

## Warren Buffet: The Confidence of Calculated Risks

Warren Buffet, the Oracle of Omaha, has a different take on confidence. His investment philosophy is grounded in meticulous research and a thorough understanding of business fundamentals. Buffet once remarked, "Risk comes from not knowing what you're doing."

In Buffet's view, confidence is not about ignoring risks; it's about understanding them so well that you can navigate them effectively. This form of confidence is less flashy than Musk's but equally impactful. It's the confidence of a chess master, carefully planning several moves ahead.

## Bill Gates: The Assurance of Lifelong Learning

Bill Gates, the co-founder of Microsoft, represents another facet of confidence-continuous learning. He has consistently emphasized the importance of lifelong learning and adapting to new challenges. Gates said, "As we look ahead into the next century, leaders will be those who empower others."

Gates' confidence comes from his relentless pursuit of knowledge and belief in empowering others. It's a quieter form of confidence, one that is focused

# Chapter Forty

# Confidence Continued

In business and personal achievement, confidence is often an overlooked yet critical element that separates the extraordinary from the ordinary. Whether it's the audacity to challenge the status quo, as Elon Musk would recommend, the calculated confidence in one's expertise echoed by Warren Buffet, or the quiet assurance that comes from lifelong learning, as advised by Bill Gates, confidence serves as an underutilized co-pilot in the journey toward success.

## The Multifaceted Nature of Confidence

Confidence is not a one-size-fits-all concept; it manifests in various forms and styles. For some, it might come from years of experience and expertise, allowing them to make decisions with a level of certainty that others might find baffling. For others, it may stem from a natural inclination to take risks and challenge the existing norms. The key is understanding that confidence is versatile and can be developed in multiple ways.

## Confidence Through Vision

"Confidence through Vision" represents the leaders and individuals who dare to dream big and take the steps to realize those dreams, regardless of the odds. When Elon Musk states, "When something is important enough, you do it even if the odds are not in your favor," he encapsulates this form of audacious confidence. The vision is the driving force, and the confidence to achieve it comes from an unshakable belief in its importance.

## Confidence Through Expertise

Then there's the "Confidence through Expertise," which comes from years of experience and a deep understanding of one's domain. This form of confidence is often associated with Warren Buffet, who reminds us that "Risk comes from not knowing what you're doing." In this case, confidence is a byproduct of expertise and calculated risk-taking, helping to navigate the complex landscape of investment and business.

## Confidence Through Empowerment

Finally, "Confidence through Empowerment" is the kind that grows as one focuses on personal growth and the growth of others. Bill Gates wisely said, "As we look ahead into the next century, leaders will be those who empower others." This form of confidence comes from a place of knowledge and the desire to uplift those around you.

## Harnessing Your Own Co-pilot

As we've seen, confidence can take many forms, each valid and effective in its own right. The first step to harnessing this underutilized co-pilot is identifying which form of confidence resonates most with you.

Once that's done, the path to nurturing it becomes more apparent, allowing you to navigate challenges with a newfound sense of assurance.

## Conclusion

In summary, confidence is a versatile, multifaceted trait that can significantly influence your path to success. It's the invisible hand that guides you, the whisper in your ear that says you can do it, and the foundation upon which you build your dreams. By understanding and adopting the correct form of confidence, you put yourself in the cockpit of your life, ready to take off toward your goals.

## Harnessing Your Own Co-Pilot (Continued)

Embarking on the journey to cultivate your own brand of confidence begins with self-awareness. You need to know where you stand before understanding where you wish to go. The process might start with identifying your strengths and acknowledging your weaknesses, setting the stage for improvement and growth.

## Self-Assessment

A good starting point is to engage in self-assessment exercises. These could range from personality tests to professional development reviews or informal discussions with mentors and colleagues. The objective is to get a 360-degree view of your capabilities and limitations. Once you've gathered this data, you can move forward with a focused strategy to bolster your confidence.

## Building a Confidence Portfolio

Like an investor maintains a diversified portfolio, consider developing a 'Confidence Portfolio.' This portfolio could contain elements such as your skills, accomplishments, and positive feedback from others. Whenever you need a confidence boost, revisit this portfolio. Over time, you'll find that this collection serves as a tangible reflection of your growth and capabilities.

## The Role of Failure

Failure is an often overlooked but crucial ingredient in the recipe for confidence. Every setback offers a lesson, and each lesson serves as a stepping stone to greater self-assurance. Elon Musk's audacity to challenge the norms didn't come without its share of failures, yet each one only strengthened his resolve. Embracing failure as an opportunity for learning can shift your perspective and enhance your confidence.

## Networking and Mentorship

Warren Buffet's calculated approach to risks is not a solitary endeavor; it's backed by years of learning from mentors and networking with industry experts. Surrounding yourself with knowledgeable and supportive people can provide a safety net of advice and guidance, adding another layer to your confidence.

## The Virtuous Cycle of Confidence

As you grow more confident, you'll find that this self-assurance spills over into other aspects of your life, creating a virtuous cycle. For example, Bill Gates' confidence in his knowledge and his focus on empowerment contribute to a cycle where confidence begets success, which, in turn, begets more confidence.

## The Limitations of Confidence

While confidence can be a mighty co-pilot, it is essential to recognize its limitations. Overconfidence can lead to poor decision-making and an underestimation of the risks involved. Balance is key, and this is where the wisdom of Warren Buffet's cautionary approach can serve as a guiding principle.

## Mindfulness and Continuous Growth

Bill Gates' perspective on empowering others extends to oneself as well. Practicing mindfulness and knowing your own growth journey can keep your confidence grounded. Being a lifelong learner not only equips you with the tools to succeed but also keeps your confidence rooted in reality.

## Conclusion

Confidence is more than just a feeling; it's a skill that can be honed and developed over time. Whether you resonate with the audacity of Elon Musk, the calculated risk-taking of Warren Buffet, or the quiet empowerment advocated by Bill Gates, the common thread is that confidence, in whatever form, can be your underutilized co-pilot guiding you to your destination. Understanding your unique style of confidence and actively nurturing it can pave the way for personal and professional success. It's about taking the reins of your life, guided by an unwavering belief in your abilities.

# Chapter Forty-One

# Experience, Insight, and Control

As we touched upon the multifaceted nature of confidence in the previous chapter, exploring the elements that serve as the building blocks of that confidence becomes imperative. In this context, three critical factors come into play: experience, insight, and control. These elements contribute to your self-assurance and serve as the pillars that uphold it.

## Experience: The Road Well-Traveled

The first cornerstone is experience—your history of interactions, decisions, and outcomes. Experience is the teacher that offers lessons in both success and failure. With each experience, you better understand your capabilities, limitations, and world. This understanding, in turn, enhances your confidence, giving you the assurance to navigate complexities with greater ease.

## Learning from Experience

The key is not merely to collect experiences like badges but to learn from them. Whether a successful venture or a failed project, each experience offers invaluable lessons contributing to your overall growth. The more adept you become at learning from these experiences, the more nuanced your understanding becomes, further fueling your confidence.

## Insight: The Wisdom to Discern

Insight is your ability to dissect situations, understand underlying patterns, and make informed decisions. This quality is not purely innate; it's honed over time through reflection, education, and interaction. Insight allows you to approach problems critically, enabling you to foresee potential outcomes and make decisions accordingly.

## The Role of Emotional Intelligence

Insight also encompasses emotional intelligence—the skill to understand not only situations but people. Being in tune with your own emotions and those of others can significantly enhance your insight, adding another layer to your confidence. This balanced emotional awareness enables you to interact more effectively with people, whether in personal relationships or professional settings.

## Control: The Rudder of Your Ship

The third pillar, control, is your ability to influence outcomes. While you can't control every variable, having a sense of control over your actions and their consequences is empowering. This control is often a direct outcome of experience and insight; the more you have of these two, the better your ability to steer your life in the desired direction.

## The Illusion of Control

It's important to note that control is often more about perception than reality. The belief that you have control can be as empowering as actually having it. However, this should not slip into overconfidence. The aim is to find the right balance, where you exert control where possible but also acknowledge the limitations of your influence.

## Conclusion

Experience, insight, and control are the scaffolding upon which your confidence is built. Each contributes to a robust sense of self-assurance that equips you to face challenges and seize opportunities.

As you cultivate these three pillars, you'll find that your confidence becomes your most reliable co-pilot, guiding you through the ever-changing landscape of life's complexities.

## The Role of Emotional Intelligence (Continued)

Emotional intelligence goes beyond recognizing emotions; it involves the nuanced skill of regulating those emotions and leveraging them for constructive purposes. For instance, staying calm under pressure directly results from high emotional intelligence. This emotional control fosters a deeper sense of self-assurance, allowing you to operate confidently even when faced with high-stress situations.

## Building Emotional Resilience

One aspect of emotional intelligence that significantly impacts confidence is emotional resilience—the ability to bounce back from setbacks. Emotional resilience strengthens your capacity to maintain control in challenging circumstances, bolstering your confidence. It's about adopting a proactive rather than a reactive stance, treating setbacks as learning opportunities rather than defeats.

## The Intersection of Experience and Insight

Experience and insight are deeply interconnected. Your experiences feed into your insights, and your insights, in turn, shape how you approach new experiences. This cyclical relationship is a dynamic engine for building confidence. When you apply your insights to new situations and gain additional experience, you create a positive feedback loop that continually enriches your understanding and self-assurance.

## The Power of Adaptability

In a rapidly changing world, adaptability is not just a useful trait but a necessary one. The confidence to adapt comes from a blend of experience, insight, and control. When you're adaptable, you react to changes and proactively engage with them. This proactive engagement gives you greater control over the situation, significantly boosting your confidence.

## Confidence as an Outcome

While we often consider confidence a prerequisite for tackling challenges, it's also an outcome. Each time you successfully navigate a difficult situation, your confidence grows. It serves as the fuel for your journey and the reward at the end. This dual role makes confidence indispensable to your personal and professional development arsenal.

## Control Through Delegation

Control doesn't always mean handling everything yourself; it can also mean knowing when to delegate. Understanding your strengths and weaknesses enables you to allocate tasks effectively in personal projects or a team setting. This form of control is a manifestation of your experience and insight and serves to solidify your confidence further.

## The Role of External Factors

While experience, insight, and control are internal factors that contribute to confidence, it's crucial to acknowledge the role of external factors. Supportive relationships, constructive feedback, and a conducive environment can all serve as catalysts for building confidence. Surrounding yourself with positivity can provide an additional layer of assurance, making your journey toward greater confidence smoother.

## Long-term Vs. Short-term Confidence

It's important to distinguish between long-term and short-term confidence. Short-term confidence might be task-specific and transient, but long-term confidence is a stable trait you carry with you across different aspects of your life. Building long-term confidence requires a sustained effort to develop experience, insight, and control.

## Conclusion

In the grand scheme of personal and professional growth, experience, insight, and control serve as the sturdy pillars that hold up the edifice of your confidence. By consciously cultivating these three elements, you are setting up a robust framework that supports your current endeavors and prepares you for future challenges. In this way, confidence becomes both your co-pilot and your destination, guiding you through the complexities of life while continually evolving alongside you.

While starting at the bottom gives you a unique perspective, it doesn't automatically equip you with the skills to lead effectively. Companies must recognize this gap and invest in comprehensive leadership training programs. An organization's future depends on its leaders and how well they can inspire and guide their teams toward collective success.

# Chapter Forty-Two

# Building a Trustworthy Team

Building a trustworthy team is one of the most crucial aspects of effective leadership. A team that trusts its leader is more engaged, motivated, and productive. But how does one go about building a trustworthy team? It starts with the leader.

As a leader, your actions set the tone for the team. If you want to build trust, you need to be trustworthy yourself. This means being honest, transparent, and consistent in your actions. Nothing erodes trust faster than inconsistency and hidden agendas.

Additionally, you need to create an environment where everyone feels valued and heard. This includes being open to feedback, encouraging open communication, and actively listening to what your team members have to say. When people feel like they can speak freely without fear of reprisal, it fosters a culture of trust and collaboration.

But building a trustworthy team isn't just about what the leader does; it's also about the team's composition. A strong, cohesive team is built on diversity- not just in terms of ethnicity or gender but also in skills, experiences, and perspectives.

This diversity can enrich the team's collective knowledge and problem-solving abilities, leading to better outcomes.

It's also essential to set clear expectations from the outset. Trust is built on the foundation of shared goals and mutual understanding. When everyone knows what is expected of them and what they can expect from others, it creates a stable framework within which trust can grow.

Building trust is not a one-time activity but an ongoing process. It requires constant nurturing and reinforcement. As a leader, you must continuously monitor the team dynamics, address issues promptly, and give credit where it's due. Recognizing and rewarding trustworthiness will not only strengthen the existing trust but also encourage its proliferation within the team.

In summary, building a trustworthy team starts with being a trustworthy leader. From setting the right tone and creating an open environment to choosing the right team members and setting clear expectations, every action you take contributes to the level of trust within the team. It's a long-term investment that will pay off manifold in terms of productivity, employee satisfaction, and organizational success.

# Chapter Forty-Three

# Building a Trustworthy Team (Cont'd)

One of the most overlooked aspects in building a trustworthy team is the concept of 'psychological safety.' Coined by Harvard Business School professor Amy Edmondson, psychological safety refers to a climate where team members feel safe to take risks, voice their opinions, and admit mistakes without fear of humiliation. Leaders must strive to cultivate this within their teams.

Creating a psychologically safe environment starts with leaders admitting their mistakes and vulnerabilities. This sets a precedent for team members, showing them that it's okay to be imperfect. Additionally, leaders should encourage open discussions, even debates, as long as they are constructive and lead to problem-solving.

Moreover, trust isn't a static element; it's dynamic and fluctuates with time and actions. Leaders must remember this and strive to maintain and rebuild trust when it's broken. This includes transparent communication, especially during challenging times. When team members see their leader navigating difficulties with honesty and resilience, their trust deepens.

Let's not forget the role of empathy in leadership. Empathy allows you to understand the individual motivations of your team members, which is crucial for creating a trustworthy environment. This doesn't mean you have to agree with everyone's point of view, but understanding where they're coming from can significantly improve team dynamics.

In summary, trust is the cornerstone of effective leadership and team performance. Building and maintaining it requires consistent efforts, transparency, and the courage to be vulnerable. It's an ongoing process that pays off significantly in the long run, leading to higher productivity, improved employee satisfaction, and, ultimately, organizational success.

# Chapter Forty-Four

# AI and the Future of Leadership: Bridging the Skills Gap and Navigating Regulation

Artificial Intelligence (AI) is not just a buzzword; it's a transformative force reshaping industries, economies, and the essence of human interaction. This chapter will delve into the complexities of leading in an AI-dominated world, exploring how to bridge the emerging skills gap and navigate the murky waters of regulation.

## The Transformative Power of AI: A New Leadership Paradigm

AI's influence on modern business is monumental. Whether it's automating routine tasks, analyzing vast amounts of data, or engaging with customers in new ways, AI is a game changer. For leaders, this means adapting to a new paradigm where human and machine collaboration is the norm. This transformation presents challenges and opportunities for optimizing productivity, efficiency, and innovation.

## The Skills Gap: The Race to Adapt

The increasing integration of AI into organizational processes has resulted in a widening skills gap. Employees need to understand their specific roles and how AI influences their tasks and responsibilities. The challenge for leaders is dual: up-skilling the existing workforce while attracting new talent proficient in AI and data analytics. Failure to address this gap could result in lost opportunities and reduced competitive advantage.

## Regulatory Landscape: A Maze of Complexity

With the growing influence of AI comes increased scrutiny and the need for regulation. Leaders must grapple with ethical considerations, data privacy issues, and the potential for AI misuse. As regulations evolve, staying compliant will require constant vigilance and adaptability. Leaders must be proactive in understanding not just the current regulatory landscape but also potential future changes that could impact their operations.

## Adaptability: The Cornerstone of Modern Leadership

The ability to adapt is becoming increasingly crucial in an AI-dominated world. Leaders must be agile and willing to pivot strategies quickly in response to technological advancements. This requires fostering a culture of continuous learning and innovation within the organization. Training programs, workshops, and seminars can keep the workforce updated and aligned with the company's AI initiatives.

## Age and AI: The Double-Edged Sword

The multi-generational makeup of the modern workforce can be both a challenge and an asset in the age of AI. While younger generations may quickly adapt to new technologies, older employees offer invaluable experience that can contextualize AI data and insights. Leaders can capitalize on this by creating mentorship programs that encourage knowledge sharing across age groups and enrich the organization's skill set.

## The Future: Navigating the Uncharted Territory of AI

As we hurtle toward a future where AI is ubiquitous, the role of a leader becomes increasingly intricate. While the path is fraught with challenges, it also offers unprecedented opportunities for growth and innovation. Leaders who embrace the complexities of AI, invest in bridging the skills gap, and keep a vigilant eye on regulatory changes are the ones who will successfully navigate this uncharted territory.

## Conclusion: The Leader as the Captain of the AIShip

In the AI-dominated landscape, leaders are the captains steering their organizations through turbulent yet exciting waters. They must be adept at maneuvering through the complexities of technological advancements, regulatory changes, and workforce up-skilling.

By adopting a proactive and adaptive approach, they can successfully harness the transformative power of AI to create a prosperous and ethical future.

# Chapter Forty-Five

# The Symbiosis of Leadership and Technology: Charting the Course for the Future

As we stand at the precipice of a new era, the fusion of leadership and technology becomes not just a trend but a necessity. This chapter serves as a culminating reflection on the symbiotic relationship between leadership and technology, aiming to inspire a sense of wonder and anticipation for the future.

## The Inevitable Fusion: Leadership Meets Technology

Leadership and technology are no longer separate entities but are intertwined in a complex dance that defines the modern business landscape. As we have seen in the preceding chapters, whether it's managing a multi-generational workforce, navigating the intricacies of AI, or adapting to rapid technological changes, modern leaders must wear many hats. They are not just decision-makers but also innovators, ethicists, and lifelong learners.

## The Future Leader: A Polymath in the Digital Age

The future leader will be a polymath, proficient in business acumen, technological understanding, ethical reasoning, and human psychology. This multidisciplinary approach will be essential for navigating the challenges and opportunities of the future. The advent of technologies like quantum computing, augmented reality, and blockchain will require leaders to learn and adapt constantly.

## The Ethics of Innovation: A Balancing Act

Ethical considerations will take center stage as technology advances at a breakneck pace. Leaders will be tasked with ensuring that innovation does not come at the cost of ethical compromises or social inequality. The role of a leader will thus expand to include that of a moral compass, guiding not just their organization but also contributing to societal well-being.

## The Global Leader: Navigating Cultural and Technological Landscapes

The future is global, and leaders must be prepared to navigate technological and cultural complexities. With the rise of remote work and international teams, understanding cultural differences and leveraging them for organizational success will become a crucial leadership skill.

## The Human Element: technology as an Enabler, not a Replacement

Despite the rapid advancements in AI and automation, the human element remains irreplaceable. Leaders must remember that technology is an enabler, not a substitute for human skills, creativity, and judgment. The challenge lies in harmonizing human skills with technological capabilities to create a synergistic environment that drives innovation and productivity.

## Conclusion: A Tribute to the Visionaries

As we conclude this exploratory journey into the future of leadership, it's essential to pay tribute to the visionaries who have guided us through this complex landscape. To Don Jones, whose insightful perspectives have laid the foundation for this discourse, and to Contributing Writer Corky Reams, whose articulate expressions have enriched this narrative, we owe a debt of gratitude. Together, they have crafted a tapestry that not just informs but

# Chapter Forty-Six

# I Think the Wiring Is Wrong

Electrical wiring provides a safe and efficient pathway for electrical currents to supply devices and appliances with power. Proper wiring is vital to ensure safety, prevent fire hazards, and guarantee the optimal operation of electrical systems.

## Basics of Electrical Wiring

A. Wire Types

- Conductors: Typically, copper or aluminum facilitates the flow of electrical current.

- Insulators: Plastic or rubber coatings that protect against electric shock and short circuits.

B. Color Coding

- Distinguishes between different wire functions and prevents misconnection.

C. Importance of Correct Wiring

- Safety: Prevents electrical shocks, short circuits, and fire hazards.

- Equipment Integrity: Protects appliances and devices from damage due to improper power supply.

- Energy Efficiency: Ensures optimal operation and reduces unnecessary energy consumption.

1. Wiring Practices

- Correct Wire Sizing: Choosing appropriate wire gauges prevents overheating and energy loss.

- Proper Connections: Ensuring tight and correct connections to prevent arcs and loose wires.

- Grounding: A crucial practice to prevent electrical shock by providing a path for fault currents.

1. Professional Involvement: Utilizing trained electricians ensures adherence to local codes and regulations.

- Quality Assurance: Ensures the wiring is safe, secure, and high-quality.

- Troubleshooting: Professionals can identify and rectify issues effectively and safely.

I just provided you with the basic knowledge, understanding, and importance of wiring. In addition, I think you would concur that attempting to operate in this arena without proper knowledge is unwise and unsafe. Without understanding and training, you would not attempt to take on a wiring project. Well, let's put it this way: if you were in your conscious mind, you would not try to take on an electrical project without the knowledge and training.

What if I told you people are wired differently? Yes, we are a mass of energy, and things can go wrong if we are not properly managed. For example, you would not wire a refrigerator like a toaster oven. Yes, they are both appliances—but wired differently. If you hear a leader say they manage everyone the same, please step away from them as they have not been adequately trained on dealing with energy (people). You don't want that negative currency passing on to you.

When dealing with people, we must learn to manage personalities, not the business. You will graduate as a Certified People Leader (CPL) when you acquire that knowledge. Managing people is not about having the proper gravitas or tenure on the job. It's about understanding how people are wired and what currency is required to get them plugged into the job with energy and passion for what they are doing.

I challenge you to think differently. Instead of identifying an individual's opportunities, what if you came up with ideas that can help an individual become better rather than how you hold them accountable?

Before you question this notion, I get it. Sometimes, someone needs to be held accountable, such as violating a policy or procedure or extreme tardiness. I could name a few more examples here for termination, but you get it. All I am saying is that ideas are more powerful than talking about people.

What ideas do you have in mind for making them better?

It was Socrates who said, "Strong minds discuss ideas, average minds discuss events and weak minds discuss people."

There is a hollow path to victory without a community mindset. The question becomes, are you plugged into a community mindset as a leader? It doesn't matter the size of the building; what matters is togetherness.

Winning is about togetherness. Try accomplishing anything without it. The hidden secret is in plain sight.

Many leaders will try implementing all types of algorithms or theses without success. We are simply overthinking the obvious. When things get hard, we must strive toward unity.

Many organizations will double down on isolating individuals and applying pressure when times are tough in a bad economy. This will often weaken the tribe rather than strengthen it. You see this play out in nature.

Transformation is not for everyone. Transformation requires a mental move that many individuals or corporations are unwilling to risk. Transformation requires a move from your heart but also in your mind. A shift is needed within your thought life to suppress the inner blockage and distractions.

As leaders, we sometimes think we'll create a positive work environment by asserting more authority and power. But it's quite the opposite of following the behaviors of great leaders. The only way we have a healthy environment is by creating it.

When it seems like we are losing momentum in the workplace, a natural reaction might be to stand up more, raise your voice more, and be more expressive with your actions. But try to establish a demeanor of peace before engaging in the situation. It will most likely feel uncomfortable at first and may take time to get used to, but ultimately, you'll be modeling how to create a healthy environment as great leaders always do.

Here's what's most important: avoid standing in two places; that's where doubt is most effective. Instead, decide to stand in one place where trust is most effective.

Allow me to level up here. I'm just like any average leader on any given day. I can go from doubt when things get tough to trusting the process when the chaos subsides. However, I never prescribe to getting angry. Anger is not necessarily the issue; controlling or managing our anger is imperative. I'm not telling you not to be angry. I encourage you to consider how your anger affects individuals and the people we manage.

Controlling your inner emotional thoughts will grant you wisdom and clarity of the situation. Most individuals don't begin with the end in mind but rather begin only to regret their actions later. However, there are no refunds for regrets. We must live with our fast-acting thoughts. Some of our actions are recoverable, and many are not. That's the risk you must take if you are a person who lacks control of your impulsive thoughts.

Here's the sad state of affairs: Many leaders know their actions do not align with their company's core leadership values. However, they have decided to be the vanguard of polarities.

What is polarity? It is when you are clear of your actions but decide to go forward with your decision. Most people know when something is good or bad, right or wrong. They say the right things but behave differently. Just remember, when you are under the influence of adrenaline, it overrides your logical faculties. When emotions are involved, clarity of thoughts is absent.

You can decide now what type of leader you will become. When everything appears to be failing, keep humility at the forefront of your thoughts and actions. Trust in the lesson and thought processes you have learned in this chapter, and you will most likely prevail. Small beginnings can lead to significant momentum and results. Everyone has the ability to be a great leader. However, it will take a conscious, intentional cadence of deliberate actions. You cannot wish to be great; you must take the right actions.

www.ingramcontent.com/pod-product-compliance
Lightning Source LLC
LaVergne TN
LVHW021237080526
838199LV00088B/4556